The Essence of Management Accounting

THE ESSENCE OF MANAGEMENT SERIES

The Essence of Management Accounting

SECOND EDITION

LESLIE CHADWICK MBA FCCA CERT ED

Chair of Undergraduate Programmes
at the University of Bradford Management Centre

Prentice Hall

New York London Toronto Sydney Tokyo Singapore
Madrid Mexico City Munich Paris

First published 1991 by
Prentice Hall International (UK) Ltd
This edition published 1997 by
Prentice Hall Europe
Campus 400, Maylands Avenue
Hemel Hempstead
Hertfordshire HP2 7EZ
A division of
Simon & Schuster International Group

Typeset in 10/12 pt Palatino
by Photoprint, Torquay

Printed and bound in Great Britain by
TJ Press (Padstow) Ltd

Library of Congress Cataloging-in-Publication Data

Chadwick, Leslie, 1943–
    The essence of management accounting/Leslie Chadwick.
      p.   cm. — (The Essence of management series)
    Includes bibliographical references and index.
    ISBN 0–13–552340–0
    1. Managerial accounting. I. Title. II. Series.
HF5657.4.C48 1997
658. 15'11—dc20   90–20451
                                                        CIP

British Library Cataloguing in Publication Data

A British Library CIP data catalogue record is available
from the British Library

ISBN 0–13–552340–0

---

1 2 3 4 5   01 00 99 98 97

Contents

Appendix 2   Present value tables and annuity tables   161

Preface

Many of the managers and executives who attend short management accounting courses, and students involved with non-professional accountancy courses, frequently comment that:

- They don't want to become accountants.
- They have no desire to become expert in the number crunching side of accountancy.

However, they do all appear to have a good idea about what they are really looking for. I have been told on numerous occasions by managers and non-professional accountancy students that what they need to be able to do is the following:

- Acquire a good grasp of the terminology used.
- Acquire a working knowledge of the important principles and techniques.
- Understand how the figures which are produced have been arrived at, e.g. how the overhead cost of a product may be calculated.
- Know what information could be available to assist with decision making.
- Use the information which is generated.
- Know about the limitations of the information produced.
- Appreciate the way in which the information, systems and techniques may affect people, i.e. the behavioural aspects.

Changes to the Second Edition

It is against this background that the first edition was written. This second edition involved a full revision of the text, and aims at improving and updating existing material, examples and questions, and adding a little more material where appropriate. In particular, this edition includes an introductory chapter on activity-based costing (ABC) and more material on capital investment appraisal.

Readership

This book, one of the Prentice Hall Essence of Management series, has been especially written for managers and executives attending short courses, either for reading before or during the course. However, students undertaking business and management courses of a longer duration should also find the book helpful as pre-course reading or for reading during their course; e.g. it should be particularly useful for one-semester introductory level under-graduate degree courses and post-graduate courses such as the MBA.

Teaching and learning features

- ☐ Each chapter sets out the objectives which it is intended will have been achieved by the time the study of the chapter has been completed.
- ☐ The worked examples in the text, which illustrate management accounting techniques, take the reader through the process step by step.
- ☐ Integrated throughout the text are several self-assessment questions, with suggested answers given at the end of the text.
- ☐ The essence of the subject is provided in a comprehensive summary at the end of each chapter.
- ☐ Each chapter ends with some suggested further reading.

The author welcomes comments from users of this book which will be taken into account when a new edition is prepared, and would like to thank all those users who commented on the first edition.

1

Introduction to management accounting

Objectives

The principal aim of this chapter is to introduce you to the purpose and scope of management accounting. When you have completed this chapter you should be able to do the following:

□ Appreciate why predetermined cost and management accounting systems are needed.
□ Understand what is meant by elements of cost.
□ Distinguish between direct and indirect costs, and fixed and variable costs.
□ Appreciate the way in which management accounting can meet the needs of management.

The two cost and management accounting systems

Cost and management accounting systems can be divided into two, as shown in Figure 1.1. Historic costing looks back at past performance. However, it must be remembered that simply comparing current performance with past performance is not such a satisfactory way of controlling business activities.

Why not? Because it is hard to say whether or not past performance has been good, bad or indifferent.

However, management accounting tends to make extensive use of predetermined systems such as budgetary control and standard costing.

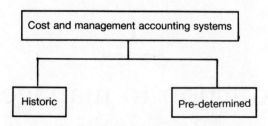

Figure 1.1   Cost and management accounting

Why? The principal reasons are as follows:

☐ A lot of the management accounting information produced is about the future. Management needs to be able to assess what its decisions/ proposed decisions will mean in terms of future costs and revenues, etc.
☐ The quest for a 'yardstick', i.e. a way of assessing and measuring performance, e.g. a sales target, budgeted expenditure on advertising, etc.

The budgets and standards used should provide targets at which to aim; they should *not* merely reflect what is expected to happen. Thus, control can be exercised by comparing the planned (budgets or standards) figures with the actual results at regular intervals.

Budgets and budgetary control are covered in Chapter 8 and standard costing is covered in Chapter 9.

The elements of cost

The cost of a product, job or service is made up of the elements of cost, i.e. materials, labour and overheads (see Figure 1.2). The last of the three (overheads) is the most difficult to deal with. Further on in this book we will take a look at all three elements. In addition to looking at the absorption (or total) costing method of dealing with overheads, we will also look at the marginal (variable) costing approach. Marginal costing is a technique which can be used for decision making purposes and is therefore an important area of study.

Figure 1.2   The elements of cost

Figure 1.3 The classification of costs

The classification of costs

Costs can be classified in a number of ways (see Figure 1.3). This simplified classification looks at just two ways of classifying costs. You will come across these terms time and time again:

☐ **Direct costs** can be identified as forming part of the product or service, e.g. manufacturing wages and raw materials which are used in the production process.

☐ **Indirect costs** are usually referred to as **overheads**, they are expenses which do not form part of the product, e.g. the wages of cleaners and canteen staff, materials used for cleaning and maintenance.

☐ **Fixed costs** have to be paid out irrespective of the level of activity, but within a relevant range and also within the short term, e.g. a three monthly or six monthly period. Examples of fixed costs are insurance of buildings, rent of premises and maintenance contracts, etc.

☐ **Variable (marginal) costs** comprise the direct costs referred to above plus variable overheads. They may be described as those costs which vary with the level of activity within a relevant range. Examples of variable costs are direct labour and direct materials plus those expenses which vary with the level of output, e.g. power for machines.

A combination of fixed and variable costs may be referred to as a **semi-variable** cost, e.g. a fixed rental for some equipment plus a variable element charged according to usage.

Costs may be further divided up between products, services, departments, sections and functions. These may be referred to as **cost centres**. A cost centre is simply a location, person or function, etc., to which costs are allocated and apportioned. The aim is to collect and accumulate the costs applicable to each specific cost centre.

What is management accounting?

Management accounting is very closely linked to cost accounting; so closely, in fact, that it is difficult to say where cost accounting ends and where management accounting begins. **Cost accounting** simply aims to measure the performance of departments, goods and services. However, **management accounting** is much, much more, and involves the following.

The provision of information for management
Indeed, the role of the management accountant could well be described as that of an 'information manager'. The information generated should be designed to assist management, to control business operations, and to help management with decision making. In fulfilling this role the management accounting department/section must consult with the users of the information, i.e. management, to assess its needs in terms of precisely what information is required and when, etc. The aim is to provide management with a flow of relevant information, e.g. reports, statements, spreadsheets, etc., as and when required. A frequent flow of information (weekly or monthly) should enable management to respond to emerging problems/situations as soon as possible. The early detection of problems = earlier solutions/early action.

Advising management
A key part of management accounting is to advise management about the economic consequences and implications of its (proposed) decisions and alternative courses of action. In particular, this advice should answer a frequently overlooked question: What happens if things go wrong? or if interest rates go up? or if the sales target is not achieved?

Forecasting, planning and control
A lot of management accounting is concerned with the future and predetermined systems such as budgetary control and standard costing. Such systems investigate the differences (i.e. variances) which arise as a result of actual performance being different from planned performance in terms of budgets or standards. In addition, the management accountant should also be involved in strategic planning, e.g. the setting of objectives and the formulation of policy. The forecasting process will involve accounting for uncertainty (risk) via statistical techniques, such as probability, etc.

Communications
If the management accounting system is to be really effective it is essential that it goes hand in hand with a good, sound, reliable and efficient communication system. Such a system should communicate

clearly by providing information in a form which the user, i.e. managers and their subordinates, can easily understand (reports, statements, tabulations, graphs and charts). However, great care should be taken to ensure that managers do not suffer from 'information overload', i.e. having too much information much of which they could well do without!

Systems
The management accounting department/section will also be actively involved with the design of cost control systems and financial reporting systems.

Flexibility
Management accounting should be flexible enough to respond quickly to changes in the environment in which the company/organization operates. Where necessary information/systems should be amended/modified. Thus, there is a need for the management accounting section/department to be involved with the monitoring of the environment on a continuing basis.

An appreciation of other business functions
Those who provide management accounting information need to understand the role played by the other business functions. In addition to communicating effectively with other business functions, they may also need to secure their co-operation and co-ordination, e.g. the budget preparation process relies on the existence of good communications, co-operation and co-ordination.

Staff education
The management accounting department/section needs to ensure that all the users of the information it provides, e.g. managers and their subordinates, are educated about the techniques used, their purpose and their benefits, etc.

'Gate keeping'
The management accounting department/section sits at a very important information junction (see Figure 1.4). This gate-keeping position places the management accounting section in a position of power; it has access to (can send information to and from) management and subordinates, and communicates with and receives a certain amount of information from the external environment. Its power arises because it can control the flow of information upwards to management or downwards to subordinates.

Limitations
Although management accounting can, and does, provide a lot of useful information, it must be stressed that management accounting is *not* an

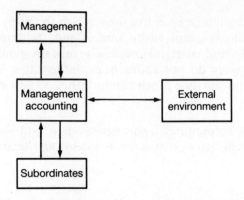

Figure 1.4 Management accounting: the gate keeper

exact science. A vast amount of the information generated depends upon subjective judgement, e.g. the assessment of qualitative factors or assumptions about the business environment. Management accounting is not the be all and end all of decision making, it is just one of the tools which can help management to make more informed decisions.

Being the servant
Finally, having established that management accounting is a tool, it must be emphasized that it is there to serve the needs of management.

Costs for decision making

The costs/revenues which need to be used for decision making purposes should be **relevant costs/revenues** (some authors refer to these as incremental costs/revenues).

Which costs and revenues are relevant to a decision? The short answer is only those costs and revenues which arise as a direct result of going ahead with the project under review. The following subsections should help you to understand which costs/revenues are relevant or irrelevant when assessing a project.

Sunk costs

Sunk costs are those costs which have already been paid out before the specific project under review was ever considered. For example, the cost of a machine purchased some time before the project was first thought of but which is to be used for the project is irrelevant. The machine will be there whether or not the project goes ahead, i.e. the money used to buy it was **sunk** at the time of its purchase. You should therefore, remember that sunk costs are irrelevant when estimating cash flows/assessing projects.

However, it is not always quite so simple!

EXAMPLE 1.1

See if you can assess the relevant costs/revenues from the following information and then compare your answer with the answer which follows:

A machine which is not being used at present, cost £120,000 six years ago, and which has a current residual value (i.e. resale value) of £25,000, would be used for the project under review. At the end of the project it would have a residual value of £7,000.

Answer

The cost of £120,000 for the machine is irrelevant. It is a sunk cost. If the project goes ahead the current residual value of £25,000 is lost, but at the end of the project £7,000 will be received. The relevant calculation is given in Table 1.1.

Table 1.1   Calculation of the relevant cost

		£
	Residual value lost	25,000
less	Residual value at the end of the project	7,000
	Relevant cost	18,000

Note that if present value tables were to be used, the £25,000 and the £7,000 would have to be dealt with separately. This aspect should become clearer to you when you study the chapter on capital investment appraisal.

Fixed costs

Fixed costs which have to be paid out whether or not a project goes ahead are irrelevant, e.g. rent of premises, insurance of buildings. However, if additional premises have to be acquired to enable a project to go ahead then the cost of those additional premises is relevant.

Labour costs

Those wages and salaries which continue to be paid whether or not a project goes ahead are irrelevant. Those which have to be paid as a result of taking on the project are relevant. Again, determining which is which is not always a simple matter.

EXAMPLE 1.2

Now see if you can identify the relevant labour costs from the following information:

If the project goes ahead the supervisor, who is currently paid £15,000 per year, will have to take on extra duties for no extra pay. Additionally, one employee currently earning £12,500 per year will have to be made redundant and paid redundancy pay of £5,600.

Answer

The amount paid to the supervisor is irrelevant to the decision. However, if extra money were paid, the extra amount would be relevant. For the redundant employee there would be a one-off relevant cost of £5,600 redundancy pay and a relevant revenue (i.e. a saving) of £12,500 per year over the life of the project.

Materials

Those which have to be purchased specially for the project are relevant.

EXAMPLE 1.3

See if you can sort out the relevant material costs from the data provided below:

Materials which are to be used for a project consist of the following:

- Material L, which cost £6,200, is already in stock. It has no further use and would cost £400 to dispose of.
- Material C, which cost £3,600, is already in stock and could be sold on the open market for £3,000.
- Material W, which has to be purchased specially for the project at £7,400.

Answer

Material L: the £6,200 is irrelevant. However, if the project went ahead there would be an incremental saving, i.e. a relevant revenue/saving, of £400 because the company would not have to dispose of it.

Material C: the £3,600 cost is irrelevant but there is an incremental loss, i.e. relevant cost of £3,000, because the material which could have been sold for the £3,000 is to be used on the project.

Material W was bought specially for the project and is a relevant/incremental cost.

Lost sales

If as a result of taking on a project, sales of other products are lost, the relevant costs/revenues will be:

sales revenue lost *less* cost of those lost sales = gross profit lost

Although sales revenue is lost, the cost of producing those goods does not have to be paid out (i.e. an incremental receipt). The net effect is a loss of gross profit.

The essence

Cost and management accounting systems

- □ **Historic** looks backwards at past events.
- □ **Predetermined** looks forward to the future.

Management accounting makes extensive use of predetermined systems such as budgetary control and standard costing.

The elements of cost

- □ Materials.
- □ Labour.
- □ Overheads.

The classification of costs

- □ Direct or indirect.
- □ Fixed or variable.

The role of management accounting

Management accounting attempts to provide managers and executives with a regular supply of relevant information which will enable them to manage more effectively, efficiently and economically. It also involves:

□ Advising management about the possible consequences of its actions.
□ Forecasting, planning and control.
□ Communications.
□ Systems.
□ Flexibility.
□ An appreciation of other business functions.
□ Staff education.
□ 'Gate keeping'.
□ Limitations.
□ Being the servant and 'information manager' of the management.

Management accounting should thus assist management with decision making and problem solving. It should help managers and executives to make the best use of their valuable time and talents in fulfilling their responsibilities and enable them to take advantage of emerging opportunities.

Costs for decision making

The estimating of cash flows and assessment of projects should use relevant/incremental costs/revenues, i.e. those that arise as a direct result of taking on the project under review. (However, what is relevant or irrelevant is not always as clear cut as you might think.)

Further reading

Drury, C., Costing: An Introduction, Chapman and Hall, 1995
Dyson, J., Accounting for Non-accounting Students, Pitman, 1994, Chapters 9, 10 and 11
Williamson, D., Cost and Management Accounting, Prentice Hall, 1996

2

Materials

Objectives

When you have worked through this chapter you should be able to do the following:

- Appreciate how the FIFO (first in, first out), LIFO (last in, first out) and AVECO (average cost) methods of pricing materials issued to production actually work.
- Also understand how they can affect product costs and stock valuations.
- Remember the kind of information which the management accounting section can produce to assist with the effective management and control of materials.
- Understand the need for management to be involved in other areas, e.g. matching, JIT (just in time), variety reduction, random stock checks, etc.

Note that it is not the objective of this chapter that you become an expert in the computational side of stock valuations. However, further reading is recommended at the end of the chapter for those who wish to delve deeper into the subject.

The valuation of materials

Materials need to be valued for the following two purposes:

- Product costs.
- Stock valuations.

There are numerous methods which may be applied for cost and management accounting purposes. We will look at three of them, which are as follows:

☐ FIFO: first in, first out.

☐ LIFO: last in, first out.

☐ AVECO: average cost.

We shall now use Example 2.1 to illustrate how they work. For each of the three methods, we can look at the calculations involved and the effect on both product costs and stock valuations.

EXAMPLE 2.1   The valuation of materials

We have been provided with the following information relating to the stock of component ZYX 3964 in 19–2:

1 April: opening stock b/f (brought forward) 500 units at £10 each.
7 April: received from suppliers 1,000 units at £12 each.
9 April: issued to production 200 units.
23 April: issued to production 400 units.

FIFO (first in, first out)

This method values the material issued to production according to the order in which it arrived, as shown in Table 2.1. It can be observed that all issues are priced at the first price of £10 until all of the 500 units opening stock, which had come in at that price, had been covered. Having dealt with the 500 opening stock units, all other issues up to the 1,000 which came in next will be priced at £12 per unit.

Table 2.1   Example of FIFO method of valuing material

19–2		Units			Value £
1 April		500	Opening stock b/f @ £10		5,000
7 April	plus	1,000	Received @ £12		12,000
		1,500	Stock in hand		17,000
9 April	less	200	Issued @ £10		2,000
		1,300	Stock in hand		15,000
				£	
			Issued 300 @ £10	3,000	
23 April	less	400	100 @ £12	1,200	4,200
		900	**Closing stock**		**10,800**
			Summary	Units	£
			Value of stock b/f and received	1,500	17,000
	less		Value of stock issued to production (£2,000 + £4,200)	600	6,200
			Value of closing stock (900 @ £12)	900	10,800

In times of rising prices this method has the effect of including the older, lower prices in the product costs and the higher, more recent prices in the stock in hand valuations. However, it does follow the order in which the stock should be physically issued, i.e. the stock should be issued in the order in which it arrived so as to avoid losses caused by ageing/deterioration.

LIFO (last in, first out)

The LIFO method values material issued to production at the most recent price as shown in Table 2.2.

The closing stock represents the 400 units which remain of the units which were purchased on 7 April at £12 per unit and the 500 opening stock units at £10 per unit, as shown in Table 2.3.

Any further issues, provided that no new stock is received, will be valued at £12 per unit up to the 400 units remaining and then at £10 per unit.

Table 2.2 Example of LIFO method of valuing material

19–2		Units		Value £
1 April		500	Opening stock b/f @ £10	5,000
7 April	plus	1,000	Received @ £12	12,000
		1,500	Stock in hand	17,000
9 April	less	200	Issued @ £12	2,400
		1,300	Stock in hand	14,600
23 April	less	400	Issued @ £12	4,800
		900	**Closing stock**	**9,800**
		Summary	Units	£
		Value of stock b/f and received	1,500	17,000
	less	Value of stock issued to		
		production (£2,400 + £4,800)	600	7,200
		Value of closing stock	900	9,800

Table 2.3 Closing stock valuation using LIFO

	£
Closing stock = 400 units at £12	4,800
500 units @ £10	5,000
	9,800

The LIFO method is not in line with the method by which the stock should be physically issued (i.e. FIFO). However, in times of rising prices, it does charge the higher, more recent prices to product costs, leaving the older, lower prices in the closing stock valuation. Thus, the product costs are more realistic and reflect current prices; however the closing stock valuation will be understated, not being at current prices.

AVECO (average cost)

With the AVECO method (see Table 2.4), all the issues and stock are valued at the average price. The average price will be recomputed every time a new batch of materials is received from suppliers.

Thus, all issues are priced at £11.33p and the closing stock is valued at £11.33p per unit. However, note that 900 units at £11.33 = £10,197, *not* £10,202. This is caused by **rounding** the average cost per unit to the nearest penny.

Table 2.4 Example of AVECO method of valuing material

19–2		Units		Value £
1 April		500	Opening stock b/f @ £10	5,000.00
7 April	*plus*	1,000	Received @ £12	12,000.00
		1,500	Stock in hand	17,000.00
9 April	*less*	200	Issued @ £11.33*	2,266.00
		1,300	Stock in hand	14,734.00
23 April	*less*	400	Issued @ £11.33	4,532.00
		900	**Closing stock @ £11.33**	**10,202.00**

* Note: The average cost $= \dfrac{£17,000}{1,500 \text{ units}} = £11.33$ (to the nearest penny).

The advantage claimed for this method is that all products, for a time, are charged for the same material at a uniform rate.

Managerial considerations

From a management point of view, you must appreciate that:

☐ With the exception of FIFO these are not methods by which materials are to be physically issued, but merely methods for the pricing of materials issued to production and for ascertaining the valuation of stocks on hand. For example, although we may use LIFO or AVECO for evaluation purposes, the materials involved should still be physically issued on a FIFO basis to avoid losses caused by the ageing process, etc.

☐ They will produce different results in terms of product costs and stock valuations, e.g. see the figures illustrated in Table 2.5.

Table 2.5 Stock valuation: comparison of product costs and
closing stock valuations

	Product costs £	Closing stock £
FIFO (£2,000 + £4,200)	6,200	10,800
LIFO (£2,400 + £4,800)	7,200	9,800
AVECO (£2,266 + £4,532)	6,798	10,202

□ The figures will be affected by price fluctuations, the quantities received and issued and the frequency of those receipts and issues.

□ There are other methods which can be used, e.g. standard cost or replacement cost.

Materials management

Stocks (also called **inventory**) of raw materials, fuels, work in progress and finished goods represent capital tied up. To make the most of its capital employed therefore, management must endeavour to keep its stock levels to an acceptable minimum. To keep stocks which do not move, or move slowly, or which are at higher than required levels, is not a good investment. In addition to the capital tied up in stocks there are also expensive **holding costs**, e.g. acquisition costs, store keeping costs, insurance, handling, etc. Thus, the real cost of materials will be their purchase cost, plus the cost of the capital used to finance their purchase, and holding costs. Managers should be able to draw upon the expertise of their management accounting section. The management accounting section should be able to provide them with a lot of useful information, such as:

□ Details of maximum, minimum and re-order levels for various stock items so that they can be reviewed and revised according to orders/seasons, etc.

□ An analysis/print out of slow moving and/or obsolete stocks.

□ An analysis of material usage (direct and indirect) by jobs, products, departments, etc.

□ Details of any stocks which are surplus to requirements.

□ A 'Pareto' analysis of, say, the 20% of the stock items which account for 80% of value stock (see further reading).

□ Costings on the employment of subcontractors.

☐ Costings comparing the making or buying of a particular component.

☐ Standard costing (see Chapter 9) – variance analysis.

☐ Budget and actual comparative statements, e.g. for material usage (see Chapter 8).

Management has a duty of ensuring that there is a sound system of stock (inventory) control within the company/organization. Much of the information generated by the management accounting section should assist managers to do this. They should, however, be active in other areas which aim to reduce the value and volume of stock held.

Matching and just in time (JIT)
Matching material requirements to the production requirements could involve the scheduling of materials to arrive at the factory, say, the day before they are due to enter the production process, and the scheduling of production to be completed and delivered, say, a day or so before the delivery date.

Variety reduction
A variety reduction exercise can reduce costs; uncalled for variety is expensive. Nowadays a certain amount of variety can be achieved using differing mixes of standardized components. Management should be aware of this at the product design stage so that uncalled for variety can be eliminated from the outset.

Random stock checks
Providing personnel who are independent of responsibility for stores with the authority to carry out random stock checks should detect errors and fraud, and act as a moral deterrent. The staff involved could also carry out investigations to assess the condition of stock.

Coding and classification systems
Firms have been known to order materials from suppliers when they already have an adequate supply within their stores. This situation can arise because of a poor coding and classification system. Managers must therefore make sure that their system is satisfactory.

Monitoring
The environment in which the company/organization operates, e.g. social, political, economic, technological, etc., must be monitored on a regular basis to identify changes taking or about to take place. For example, certain information could reveal that a particular component is about to become obsolete.

The essence

The valuation of materials

There are a number of valuation methods which can be used for the pricing of materials issued to production and for stock valuation purposes.

FIFO (first in, first out)
This method prices issues to products by following the sequence in which the stock arrived. This means that the material element of the product cost is at an earlier price, whether it be lower or higher than the price at which the material concerned has subsequently been bought. The stock valuation reflects the more recent price.

LIFO (last in, first out)
The effect on product costs and stock valuations is opposite from that produced by the FIFO (first in, first out) method.

AVECO (average cost)
There are a number of variations of this method which can be used. The method which we have looked at recomputes the average cost every time a new delivery of stock is received, as follows:

$$\text{average cost} = \frac{\text{balance of stock b/f} + \text{value of new stock received}}{\text{total number of units}}$$

$$\text{e.g. } \frac{£5,000 + £12,000}{500 \text{ units} + 1,000 \text{ units}} = \frac{£17,000}{1,500 \text{ units}} = £11.33\text{p per unit}$$

Only the FIFO (first in, first out) method is in line with the recommended way in which the materials should be physically used. All other methods are, therefore, purely methods of pricing. This means that material which was bought some time ago should be issued to production in sequence (i.e. according to FIFO) but could be priced at the most/more recent prices according to LIFO (last in, first out). Yes, it does sound odd – that is why you must appreciate that the methods referred to (with the exception of FIFO) are simply methods of pricing the materials issued and of assigning values to:

□ the product costs for the material content of the product.
□ stock in hand/closing stock.

Remember that different methods of pricing are quite likely to produce significantly varying results. However, the variations will depend upon price movements, the quantities involved and the patterns of receipts and issues.

Materials management

The cost of stocks of raw materials, fuels, and the material content of work in progress and finished goods consists of:

- ☐ The capital used to purchase the materials.
- ☐ Plus the cost of the capital used.
- ☐ Plus the holding costs, e.g. overheads, acquisition costs, handling costs, etc.

Thus, for many companies/organizations vast sums of money are used to finance the holding of stocks.

Management should aim to keep its stocks at acceptable minimum levels. However, this kind of policy is sure to increase the risk of a 'stockout' which could mean failing to honour delivery promises and lost orders. Hence the words 'acceptable minimum'. Business decisions quite frequently involve such trade-offs.

A lot of management accounting information relating to materials can assist management with stock (inventory) control and decision-making, for example:

- ☐ Reviews of stock levels.
- ☐ Identifying surplus, slow moving and obsolete stocks.
- ☐ 'Pareto analysis' – there are various applications of Pareto's 80%/20% rule.
- ☐ Costing the use of subcontractors and/or make or buy decisions.
- ☐ Standard costing – variance analysis and reports.
- ☐ With budgeting, e.g. the analysis of material consumption using budget and actual comparative statements.

In addition, management should be prepared to play an active part in the following:

- ☐ Matching material requirements to production requirements and JIT (just in time) systems.
- ☐ Variety reduction programmes and product design regarding the material content.

☐ Random stock checks.

☐ Coding and classification systems.

☐ Monitoring the environment to identify threats, opportunities, strengths and weaknesses in the materials area.

Further reading

Harper, W.M., *Cost and Management Accounting*, Pitman, 1995

Muhlemann, A.P., *Production and Operations Management*, Pitman, 1993 (for a review of Pareto analysis)

3

Labour

Objectives

When you have read carefully through this chapter, you should be able to appreciate the following:

- The importance of payroll analysis and idle time analysis in the provision of management accounting information.
- Some of the causes of idle (or non-productive) time.
- How attendance time can be reconciled.
- The kind of management accounting data which can be produced via incentive schemes.
- What is meant by 'labour turnover'.
- Which costs should be included in the cost of labour turnover.
- What management can do to reduce the cost of labour turnover.
- The need for information about recent and future developments in the labour market.

Payroll analysis

One of the principal means of providing cost and management accounting information is payroll analysis. Both direct and indirect workers can record how they spend their time via time sheets, clock cards and computer terminals, etc.

Direct workers will record how much time they spend producing products or working on jobs and how much of their time is non-productive (i.e. idle). Thus, payroll analysis will be able to provide labour costs per product, job, department or section. This will enable comparisons to be made with budgets and/or standards and the reporting of variances. It will also provide valuable information which should assist with the task of producing budgets for future accounting periods.

Another aspect of payroll analysis is **idle (non-productive) time analysis**. This analysis will show how many hours are lost for each reason. Some of the causes of idle time are as follows:

☐ Waiting for materials.

☐ Waiting for work.

☐ Waiting for the setter.

☐ Machine breakdown.

☐ Training a new operative.

☐ Committee meetings, etc.

To become more efficient management must strive to reduce idle (non-productive, lost) time. To do this managers must receive a continuous flow of up to date relevant data.

The attendance time of direct workers can be reconciled:

attendance time recorded = productive time recorded + idle time recorded

As mentioned earlier, indirect workers, e.g. cleaners, welfare and maintenance staff, can keep a record of how and where they spend their time. The payroll analysis will therefore include an analysis of indirect labour per department or section. This analysis should prove useful in the estimation of the predetermined indirect labour budget figure which is needed for computing departmental overhead absorption rates (see Chapter 4). The analysis of indirect labour can also be used to compare with budgeted figures for control purposes, e.g. to see if any overspending has occurred.

Incentive schemes .

The management accounting section can provide useful information relating to incentive schemes:

☐ A comparison between proposed schemes.

☐ The effects of amendments to existing schemes.
☐ Productivity records.

Management accounting is also concerned with the monitoring of existing incentive schemes.

The cost of labour turnover

Management needs to be more aware of the real cost of employing people, i.e. the cost of labour turnover.

What is labour turnover? It is the rate at which people leave an employer, and may be calculated as follows:

$$\frac{\text{number of persons leaving}}{\text{average number of persons on the payroll}} \times 100 \text{ (for, say, per month, quarter or half year)}$$

See for example, Table 3.1.

Table 3.1   The rate of labour turnover

Quarter	No. of persons who left	Average no. on payroll	Rate of labour turnover %
1	17	85	20.00
2	19	114	16.67

Which costs should be included? The short answer to this question is a lot more than you would expect to see. Labour turnover could include the following costs:

☐ Advertising vacancies.
☐ Recruitment – including the cost of drawing up job specifications and the employment of specialist recruitment agencies.
☐ Selection – interviews in terms of the personnel involved and the facilities provided, the hire of accommodation, meals, refreshments, travelling expenses, etc. Where special selection tests are used there are costs associated with their design, development, testing, monitoring, marking, administration and review.
☐ Engagement – records, medicals, special clothing and equipment needs.
☐ The personnel function – in terms of salaries, offices, fixtures, fittings and equipment and associated overheads such as light and heat, printing, stationery, telephone costs, etc.

- Training costs, e.g. induction training (courses for new employees to inform them about the company/organization and its products/ services), pre-job training in the company's/organization's own training school, courses, text books, travelling expenses, etc.

- Production costs, such as lost production of those who are supervising the work of new operatives. There is also the likelihood of a reduced level of output and a higher level of defective output from new operatives.

- Morale and motivation – these are both difficult to quantify but can have a dramatic impact upon the company/organization and its products/services.

What can be done to reduce the cost of labour turnover? Management needs to know the rate of labour turnover and the reasons why people leave. Managers should, therefore, obtain the rate of labour turnover:

- Per department or section.
- For males and females in age groups.

They need to find out why people are leaving and analyse whether the reasons are controllable or uncontrollable. This kind of information can be collected via interviews or questionnaires by the personnel department. Employees could leave for any of the following reasons:

- Pay.
- The nature of the work.
- Promotion.
- The hours.
- Working conditions.
- Relationships with superiors and/or subordinates.
- Housing and/or transport problems.
- Welfare and social considerations.
- Health.
- Moving away from the area, etc.

It can be seen that the process of employing people entails a great deal more than simply engaging them and paying them a wage or salary. There are many, many costs involved in the employment of labour. In fact, it can be said in conclusion that the cost of employing people represents a significant investment and that the cost of labour turnover is far greater than a lot of people would imagine.

Other matters

Quite recent and future developments in the labour area will continue to make demands upon the management accounting section. The implications of the following will all need to be costed, analysed, compared with appropriate data and monitored:

- [ ] Productivity deals.
- [ ] The introduction of flexitime.
- [ ] The provision of a nursery for employees' children.
- [ ] Profit sharing schemes.
- [ ] Employees' share schemes.
- [ ] Executives/designers, etc., working from home via computer links.
- [ ] Corporate incentives, e.g. holidays for sales staff, etc.

For this specific area alone it can clearly be seen why we described the management accounting function in our opening chapter as that of an information provider/manager.

The essence

Payroll analysis

The payroll can be divided into two categories.

Direct labour
Labour used to transform the raw material into finished goods, e.g. production workers. The direct labour content of a product can be ascertained via the time recording system, by e.g. time sheets, time cards and computer systems as a by-product of payroll analysis.

Indirect labour
Non-manufacturing workers, such as cleaners, welfare workers, canteen staff and maintenance personnel, can also record how they spend their time via time sheets or time cards, etc. It should therefore be possible to produce a payroll analysis for the indirect workers, per department or section, etc.

Another important part of payroll analysis is idle (non-productive) time analysis. This should direct the attention of management to the areas in which hours are being lost so that, where possible, it can introduce corrective action which should help to remedy the situation.

Payroll analysis can be a considerable help during the budget preparation period and with the setting of standards.

Management must ensure that all hours spent are accounted for; thus a reconciliation needs to take place, as follows:

productive hours + idle hours = attendance hours

Incentive schemes

Management need to be provided with information such as updates of existing schemes, comparative figures for new schemes and productivity records.

The cost of labour turnover

This is a cost which tends to be overlooked/ignored by management; but it is a cost which does/can involve huge sums of money.

$$\text{the rate of labour turnover} = \frac{\text{number of persons leaving}}{\text{average number of persons on the payroll}} \times 100$$

on, say, a monthly, quarterly or half yearly basis. It represents the rate at which employees leave a particular employer.

The costs associated with the employment of the labour force are:

☐ Administrative, e.g. advertising, recruitment, selection, engagement and the personnel function.

☐ Training, e.g. induction training, training courses, own training schools.

☐ Production, e.g. losses caused by new employees, defective production.

☐ Damage to morale and motivation.

Management needs to ensure that records are kept of why employees leave and that controllable causes are investigated if necessary. Appropriate corrective action could reduce the rate of labour turnover and the wasted investment in terms of the costs listed above.

Further thoughts

Management accounting information will be needed for both current and future developments in the labour area, e.g. to assess the impact on costs of providing nursery places for employees' children or allowing certain executives/designers, etc., to work at home via computer links. Management accounting needs to meet the information needs of the management, to supply information which will help management in its decision making. This is particularly important in the labour area, which in many industries forms a very high proportion of the cost of the finished product or service provided.

Further reading

Drury, C., *Costing: An Introduction*, Chapman and Hall, 1995
Williamson, D., *Cost and Management Accounting*, Prentice Hall, 1996

4

Absorption costing

Objectives

By the time you have finished studying this chapter, you should be able to do the following:

☐ Understand how overheads are incorporated into the cost of a job or product.

☐ Prepare an overhead distribution summary and calculate:
  (a) a machine hour rate;
  (b) a direct labour hour rate;
  (c) the cost of a job or product.

☐ Appreciate the limitations of absorption costing.

The aim of absorption costing

The principal aim of absorption costing (also called **traditional total absorption costing** or **total costing** or the **full cost method**) is to attempt to ensure that all overhead costs are covered by the revenues received. It should be mentioned here that this is *not an attempt to produce accurate costs*. It is, however, an attempt to answer the question of how much should be included for overheads in job/product costs/quotations.

Overheads

Overheads comprise the indirect expenditure of a business, i.e. that expenditure which does not form part of the product/job, and includes such costs as:

☐ **Indirect labour:** cleaners, canteen staff, security staff, supervisory staff, etc.

☐ **Indirect materials:** e.g. cleaning materials, maintenance materials, etc.

☐ **Indirect expenses:** rent, insurance of buildings, heating, lighting, etc.

The overheads can also be sub-divided into fixed overheads and variable overheads.

Cost centres

A cost centre is the name given to a unit/section to which costs are allocated and apportioned. It could be a department, a process, a function, a group of machines or a person. The aim is to arrive at a total overhead cost for each cost centre.

You may also come across the term **profit centre**. This is much the same as a cost centre, but is also revenue earning. Thus, a profit or loss for the centre can be computed.

Overhead absorption

Overhead absorption (also called **overhead recovery**) is the process of sharing out the overheads between jobs/products by means of **absorption rates/ recovery rates**, e.g. a rate per direct labour hour or a rate per machine hour.

Absorption costing differs from marginal costing (which we will look at in Chapter 5) in that it attempts to include most of the overheads in product/job costs: hence its other names, total costing or the full cost method. Marginal costing, on the other hand, includes only the variable overheads in product costs.

We will now describe how a typical absorption costing system works by reference to the absorption of overheads diagram (see Figure 4.1). Because the overheads have to be charged to jobs/products throughout the period/ year, the recovery rates must be calculated before the period/year begins, i.e. pre-determined.

OVERHEADS

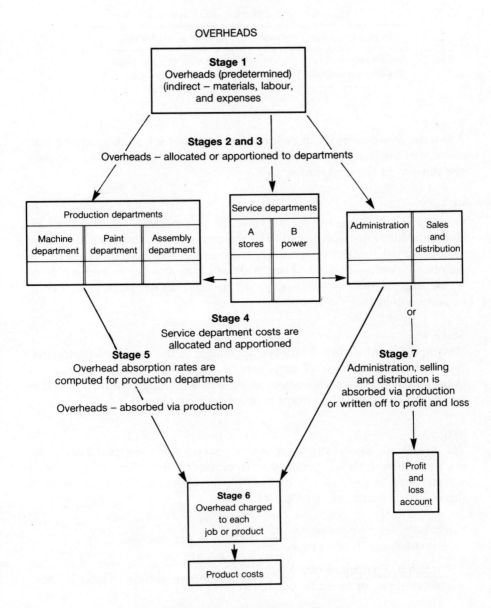

Figure 4.1 Absorption costing

Stage 1

The overheads, i.e. the indirect materials, labour and expenses have to be estimated for the forthcoming period/year.

Table 4.1 The apportionment of overheads

Item of overhead expenditure	Basis of apportionment
Rent/heating	Floor area or cubic capacity
Supervision/canteen	Number of employees

Stage 2
Those overheads which can be identified with and traced to a department/cost centre are charged to the departments/cost centres concerned, i.e. they are *allocated* to the cost centre.

Stage 3
Overheads which cannot be allocated to cost centres, i.e. those which cannot be identified and traced to departments/cost centres will have to be *apportioned* to departments/cost centres using some arbitrary basis. A number of overheads tend to *vary more with time than output* and will have to be shared out between the cost centres using some method of apportionment (see Table 4.1).

Stage 4
Having collected all the overheads applicable to the service departments, the total overhead cost of each service department can be shared out between the user departments/costs centres according to technical estimates or by using some arbitrary basis of apportionment.

Stage 5
The overhead absorption (overhead recovery) rates are calculated. The total overhead for each production department, inclusive of its share of service department costs, is divided by the estimated machine hours or direct labour hours, as appropriate:

$$\frac{\text{machine department overheads}}{\text{estimated no. of machine hours}} = \text{the rate per machine hour}$$

$$\frac{\text{paint department overheads}}{\text{estimated no. of direct labour hours}} = \text{the rate per direct labour hour}$$

There are quite a number of other overhead absorption (overhead recovery) rates which could have been used. A study of them is outside the scope of this book. I have simply opted for two of the most popular methods.

Stage 6
The overheads are then charged to products in two ways:

(a) if a job/product spends 8 machine hours in the machine department, it will be charged with 8 machine hours of overheads at the rate per machine hour.

(b) if a job/product spends 1½ direct labour hours in the paint department, it will be charged with 1½ direct labour hours of overheads at the rate per direct labour hour.

As products move from department to department they *accumulate* a portion of each department's overheads. The overheads are being recovered hour by hour, product by product.

Stage 7

The administration, selling and distribution expenses are charged either to the profit and loss account or to jobs/products. The way in which they are treated is at the discretion of the management.

The following simplified but comprehensive, example should help you to understand the process more fully.

EXAMPLE 4.1 Van Chiu Ltd

We have been provided with the information shown in Tables 4.2 and 4.3 relating to Van Chiu Ltd, for their forthcoming period. The estimated number of direct labour hours in department F was 15,500 and the estimated number of machine hours in department G was 22,500.

Table 4.2 Van Chiu Ltd: estimated overhead expenditure

Estimated overhead expenses	£	Allocation or apportionment
Indirect materials and labour:		
Production department F	9,925	Allocation
Production department G	7,900	Allocation
Service department H	15,875	Allocation
Service department I	7,300	Allocation
Rent of buildings	24,000	Floor area
Insurance of buildings	3,000	Floor area
Supervision	28,000	Number of employees
Repairs and renewals	18,000	Technical estimate: F 30%, G 50%, H 10%, I 10%
Depreciation of machinery:		
Production department F	4,000	Allocation
Production department G	9,000	Allocation
Service department H	5,000	Allocation
Service department I	2,000	Allocation
	134,000	

Table 4.3 Van Chiu Ltd: apportionment data

	F	G	H	I
Area (in square metres)	250	600	100	50
Number of employees	17	10	3	2
Technical estimates for service departments				
The use of service H	60%	30%	–	10%
The use of service I	25%	75%	–	–

1. Prepare a departmental overhead summary and calculate a direct labour hour rate for department F and a machine hour rate for department G.
2. Prepare a quotation for a job, number WW658, to which the following data are applicable:

    (a) direct material: £394;
    (b) direct labour:
        department F: 6 hours at £8 per hour;
        department G: 2 hours at £9 per hour;
        machine hours in department G were 5.
    The company uses a mark up of 30% on cost.

Answer

Having been provided with the predetermined overheads, we can prepare the departmental overhead summary in which we allocate and apportion the overheads to departments/cost centres. When this has been completed, we then share out the service department costs between user departments according to the technical estimates supplied. This will take us up to the point of having total overhead figures for departments F and G. See Table 4.4 for the overhead distribution summary.

We now know the total overhead which has been allocated and apportioned to production departments F and G, and the overhead absorption (recovery) rates for the two departments can now be calculated. The rate for production department F is:

$$\frac{\text{overheads}}{\text{direct labour hours}} = \frac{£62,000}{15,500} = £4 \text{ per direct labour hour}$$

For production department G it is:

$$\frac{\text{overheads}}{\text{machine hours}} = \frac{£72,000}{22,500} = £3.20 \text{ per machine hour}$$

The quotation for the job WW658 can now be prepared, and is as shown in Table 4.5.

Comments

You should note that the quotation for the job WW658 is made up of four elements:

Table 4.4 Van Chiu Ltd: overhead distribution summary

Overhead	Allocation or apportionment	Total £	Production departments		Service departments	
			F £	G £	H £	I £
Indirect materials and labour	Allocated	41,000	9,925	7,900	15,875	7,300
Rent and insurance	Floor area	27,000	6,750 (25%)	16,200 (60%)	2,700 (10%)	1,350 (5%)
Supervision	No. of employees	28,000	14,875 (17/32)	8,750 (10/32)	2,625 (3/32)	1,750 (2/32)
Repairs and renewals	Technical estimates	18,000	5,400 (30%)	9,000 (50%)	1,800 (10%)	1,800 (10%)
Depreciation	Allocated	20,000	4,000	9,000	5,000	2,000
		£134,000	40,950	50,850	28,000	14,200
Service H	Technical estimates		16,800 (60%)	8,400 (30%)	−28,000	2,800 (10%)
						17,000
Service I	Technical estimates		4,250 (25%)	12,750 (75%)	−	−17,000
		£134,000	£62,000	£72,000		

Table 4.5 Quotation for job WW658

		£
Direct materials		394
Direct labour	£	
(6 × £8) Department F	48	
(2 × £9) Department G	18	66
Overheads		
Department F 6 hrs @ £4	24	
Department G 5 hrs @ £3.20	16	40
Cost		500
add mark up @ 30%		150 (profit)
		650

- Direct materials.
- Direct labour.
- Overheads.
- Mark up/profit.

The direct materials and direct labour were given, but you should remember that they also will have to be predetermined/estimated in practice.

Finally, note that for department G the hours used to arrive at the overhead cost of £16 were the 5 machine hours, *not* the direct labour hours. Why? Because the overheads for that department are being recovered using a machine hour rate.

Now see if you can solve a similar problem in order to firmly fix the overhead absorption process in your mind, before we take a look at the limitations of absorption costing.

 SELF-ASSESSMENT QUESTION 4.1

Throngfirth Manufacturing

Throngfirth Manufacturing operates three production departments: the machine department, paint department and assembly department, and two service departments: stores and power. The budgeted overheads for the forthcoming period are as shown in Table 4.6.

They have also supplied you with the information given in Table 4.7, which should help you to apportion those overheads which cannot be allocated to departments.

From the data provided in Tables 4.6 and 4.7 you are required to:

1. Prepare a departmental overhead summary and calculate a machine hour rate for the machine department and direct labour hour rates for the other two production departments.

2. Calculate how much product PQ will cost if it takes £1,277 of raw materials and 15 hours of machine time in the machine department, and the following direct labour costs:

Table 4.6 Throngfirth Manufacturing: budgeted overheads

	£
Indirect materials and labour:	
Machine department	36,730
Paint department	11,270
Assembly department	11,900
Stores	16,680
Power	15,120
Other overheads:	
Fuel for power department	74,000
Building Insurance	5,800
Lighting	3,800
Supervision	19,000
Machinery Insurance	4,800
Canteen	24,200
Depreciation:	
Machine department	12,400
Paint department	6,300
Assembly department	2,100
Stores	1,400
Power	3,500
	249,000

Table 4.7 Throngfirth Manufacturing: apportionment data

	Machine department	Paint department	Assembly department	Stores	Power
Floor area (m²)	8,000	2,000	4,000	1,000	1,000
Number of employees	6	2	8	2	2
Value of machinery (£000)	75	25	–	–	25
Direct labour hours	6,400	5,000	8,000		
Machine hours	20,000	–	–		
Stores usage (technical estimate)	25%	25%	40%	–	10%
Power usage (technical estimate)	60%	25%	15%	–	–

(a) machine department: 4 hours @ £9 per hour;
(b) paint department: 3 hours @ £8 per hour;
(c) assembly: 16 hours @ £7 per hour.

3. Calculate the proposed selling price if a mark up of 40% on cost is used.

The answers are to be found on pages 139–141.

The limitations of absorption costing

The first limitation of absorption costing is the *accuracy of the predetermined overheads*. You should not lose sight of the fact that the overheads which are used are only estimates.

The selection of the bases of apportionment, e.g. floor area, number of employees, etc., depends upon the judgement of whoever has to make the selection. Different people could adopt differing bases of apportionment for the same type of expense, e.g. the rent of premises could be shared out according to floor area or cubic capacity.

There are many different methods which can be used for dealing with the distribution of service department costs (some texts refer to this process as the re-allocation of service department costs) to user departments. For example, the stores cost could be shared between user departments/cost centres according to the number of issue notes (material requisitions). However, although this may seem a reasonable and appropriate method, you should note that it does not take account of the value, weight or size of the materials.

Another problem arises because the *machine hours for the period also have to be estimated*.

Thus, when the actual figures become available:

☐ The overheads may be more or less than those which were estimated for the period.

☐ The machine hours and/or direct labour hours may be greater or lower than those which were estimated for the period.

This means that there will be either an *over- or under-absorption of overheads* charged to products. However, we cannot go back and rework the costs of the jobs/products, for they are now history. The over- or under-absorption will have to be allowed for in the profit and loss account. We will look at this aspect in a little more depth when we cover absorption costing v. marginal costing in Chapter 6.

You should also note that the treatment of administration, selling and distribution overheads and research and development expenditure varies; they can be included in the job/product costs or charged direct to the profit and loss account as an expense.

It has been found that certain companies who did charge some of their research and development expenditure to products, tended to understate the profits earned by existing products and overstate the profits earned by the new products. As a result they discontinued some of the existing products, products which were really more profitable than the new products!

An introduction to ABC (activity-based costing), an extension of the absorption costing method will be covered in Chapter 7.

Finally, remember that all absorption costing seeks to do is to attempt to ensure that all costs are covered. It does not profess to produce accurate job or product costs.

The essence

Aims

To my mind Figure 4.1 sums up the essence of absorption costing. The overheads, i.e. indirect expenditure, both fixed and variable, have to be estimated, i.e. *predetermined* before the period to which they relate commences. Absorption costing is also called **full** or **total costing**. This tells us something about what it is attempting to do. It is attempting to ensure that all overheads (fixed and variable) are covered by including them, i.e. recovering/absorbing them, in job/product costs. The aim, therefore, is not the production of accurate job/product costs.

Overheads

Overhead/indirect cost is defined by CIMA (The Chartered Institute of Management Accountants) in the UK as 'Expenditure, labour, materials or services which cannot be economically identified with a specific saleable cost unit'.

Those overheads which can be identified and traced to a department or cost centre can be charged direct to the department or cost centre concerned, i.e. allocated. Those which cannot be identified or traced to a department or cost centre, e.g. the type of expense which is incurred on behalf of all departments/cost centres, and which tends to vary more with time than output (such as the rent of buildings and insurance of buildings) will have to be apportioned according to some arbitrary basis.

The costs of running the various service departments, such as stores and power, have to be collected and accumulated to arrive at a cost for running each service. The service department cost is then shared out between user departments via technical estimates or some other arbitrary basis.

Overheads can be analysed into groups, e.g. production, administration, selling and distribution. They can also be sub-divided into fixed overheads and variable overheads.

However, whatever the analysis or sub-division used, you should note that we are still dealing with *the same overhead/indirect costs*.

Figure 4.2   Job/product cost

Overhead absorption

In deciding which basis of apportionment (arbitrary basis) to use, the selector has to choose the method which is considered to be the most appropriate for the type of expense which has to be shared out between departments/cost centres.

Before the absorption rate can be calculated the machine hours and the direct labour hours have to be estimated for the forthcoming period. The absorption rates which we have used were selected because they reflect time; as already mentioned, a lot of overheads vary more with time than output. These rates were as follows:

$$\text{machine hour rate} = \frac{\text{machine department overheads}}{\substack{\text{number of machine hours for} \\ \text{the department concerned}}}$$

$$\text{direct labour hour rate} = \frac{\text{overheads for the department}}{\substack{\text{number of direct labour hours for} \\ \text{the department concerned}}}$$

Decisions have to be made about the treatment of administration, research and development, and selling and distribution overheads. The method of dealing with such costs is at the discretion of each individual firm.

As jobs/products pass through a department/cost centre, they in effect 'clock up' a share of that particular department's/cost centre's overheads, as dictated by the overhead absorption (recovery) rate which is being used, e.g. at so much per machine hour or so much per direct labour hour. Thus, as a job/product goes from department to department it *accumulates a share of the firm's overheads*.

Note that a job/product cost is made up of the elements shown in Figure 4.2. Some businesses use this figure plus a mark up to fix their selling price or their quotation for a job/product.

Also note that absorption costing does not and cannot provide accurate job/product costs. However, it does aim to ensure that most overheads are covered by including them, be they fixed or variable, in job/product costings, e.g. production department overheads and service department overheads as illustrated in Figure 4.1.

Services

Although the illustrations in this chapter relate to a manufacturing type of environment and internal services, those organizations which provide services, e.g. health, auditing, education, radio and television do face similar problems. They also have to cost their services and account for overheads.

Limitations

Finally, remember that absorption costing does have limitations, e.g. the accuracy of the forecast overheads, the accuracy of the estimated machine hours and direct labour hours, the selection of methods of apportionment, etc.

Further reading

Drury, C., *Costing: An Introduction*, Chapman and Hall, 1995
Harper, W.M., *Cost and Management Accounting*, Pitman, 1995

5

Marginal costing and breakeven analysis

Objectives

When you have completed your study of this chapter you should:

☐ Know how marginal costing differs from absorption costing.

☐ Understand the relationship between selling price, variable cost and the contribution.

☐ Be able to calculate the contribution and profit volume ratio and use them to calculate the breakeven point.

☐ Be able to solve problems involving profit targets and key factors.

☐ Understand and be able to prepare an elementary breakeven chart.

☐ Appreciate the limitations and drawbacks of marginal costing and breakeven analysis.

Marginal costing

Marginal costing (which is also known as **variable costing** or **direct costing** or **differential costing**) is concerned with the treatment of fixed costs and the relationship which exists between three figures: sales, variable cost and the contribution.

What is the contribution? The **contribution** is the name given to the difference between sales and variable cost in the marginal cost equation.

EXAMPLE 5.1 Contribution and profit

A product sells at £50, has a variable cost of £30 and during the period ended 30 June 19—
2,000 units were sold. Fixed costs for that period amounted to £25,000. The contribution and
profit would be calculated, as shown in Table 5.1.

Table 5.1 Marginal costing relationships

		per unit (£)	2,000 units (£)	% of sales
	Selling price	50	100,000	100
less	Variable costs	30	60,000	60
	Contribution	20	40,000	40
less	Fixed costs		25,000	
	Profit		15,000	

It can be observed from Example 5.1 that the *contribution goes towards the recovery of the fixed overheads and profit*. Marginal costing is a technique which can be used as part of the decision-making process to show the effect of changes/possible changes in demand and/or selling prices and/or variable costs. It can, for example, be used: to identify the most profitable projects, in make or buy decisions, or in deciding whether or not to accept a special contract. Variable costs include only those costs which can be identified with and traced to products, e.g. direct labour, direct materials, direct expenses and variable overheads. The fixed costs are those which cannot be identified with and traced to the products. They tend to vary more with time than output, and are treated as **period costs**. This means that the fixed costs are not included in product costs. They are simply written off, in total, against the total contribution(s) generated from the sale of all the firm's products, for the period in which they were incurred: see Table 5.2. This treatment of fixed costs also means that because they are not included in product costs they are *not carried forward into the future as part of the valuation of the stocks of work in progress and finished goods*.

Table 5.2 A multi-product environment

£000		Products				Total £
		A	B	C	D	
	Contribution	20	34	36	20	110
less	Fixed costs					78
	Profit					32

The profit volume ratio (PV ratio)

The profit volume ratio explains the relationship between the contribution and sales and is calculated as follows:

$$\frac{\text{contribution}}{\text{sales}} \times 100 \text{ or } \frac{\text{contribution per unit}}{\text{selling price per unit}} \times 100$$

Using the figures in Table 5.1 this works out as:

$$\frac{£40,000}{100,000} \times 100 = 40\%$$

Yes, you may have observed that this has already been shown in Table 5.1. It is simply the contribution expressed as a percentage of sales. We now have enough information to calculate the **breakeven point**, *the point at which sales revenue and costs are equal.*

$$\frac{\text{fixed costs}}{\text{contribution per unit}} = \text{breakeven point in units}$$

$$\frac{£25,000}{£20} = 1,250 \text{ units}$$

To convert this to the breakeven point in terms of value, we just multiply the 1,250 units by the unit selling price of £50:

1,250 units × £50 = £62,500

Or we could calculate the breakeven point using the profit volume ratio, as follows:

$$\text{Fixed cost} \div \text{PV ratio} = £25,000 \times \frac{100}{40} = £62,500$$

The contribution table

A good way of dealing with problems involving changes in selling prices and/or variable costs is to construct a contribution table (see Table 5.4). The table shows the effect of the change or changes on the contribution.

EXAMPLE 5.2 The effect of change on the contribution

Using the figures from Table 5.3 as our starting point, we can work out the effects of different strategies for the forthcoming period (see Table 5.4).

Table 5.3 Strategic alternatives

	Selling price per unit £	Variable cost per unit £	Demand (units)	Fixed costs £
Current period	50	30	2,000	25,000
Strategy 1	Increase by £5	No change	1,800	28,000
Strategy 2	No change	Reduce by £3	2,500	35,000
Strategy 3	No change	Increase by £2	2,200	28,000

Table 5.4 Contribution table

		Current period	1	2	3
		£	£	£	£
	Selling price (per unit)	50	55	50	50
less	Variable cost (per unit)	30	30	27	32
	Contribution (per unit)	20	25	23	18
	Units sold demand	2,000	1,800	2,500	2,200
	Total contribution	40,000	45,000	57,500	39,600
less	Fixed costs	25,000	28,000	35,000	28,000
	Profit	15,000	17,000	22,500	11,600

It can be seen that Strategy 2 will generate the highest profit in the forthcoming period, provided the forecast demand materializes.

It should be apparent, from a Study of Example 5.2, that a movement in either the selling price or variable cost will be reflected by a movement in the contribution, as follows:

□ An increase in the selling price or a decrease in the variable cost will result in an increase in the contribution.

□ Vice versa, a decrease in the selling price or an increase in the variable cost will bring about a decrease in the contribution.

Note also that the fixed costs may vary, e.g. if the decision is taken to purchase a new machine, the fixed machine cost will increase.

Profit targets

If management sets a profit target, all you have to do is remember that the contribution is equal to the *fixed costs plus profit* (see Figure 5.1). Adding the fixed costs which have to be covered to the profit target will give you the total contribution which must be generated. The total contribution required must then be divided by the contribution per unit. This tells you how many units will have to be sold in order to generate the required contribution:

$\dfrac{\text{contribution required}}{\text{contribution per unit}}$ = the number of units which must be sold in order to generate the contribution required

$$
\begin{array}{c}
\text{Fixed costs} \\
\textit{plus} \text{ Profits or } \textit{less} \text{ Loss} \\
= \\
\text{Contribution required}
\end{array}
$$

Figure 5.1 The contribution required

EXAMPLE 5.3　Generating the required contribution

Using the current period information in Table 5.4, and assuming management has set a target profit of £24,000, we can work out how many units we would have to sell to achieve this (see Table 5.5).

Table 5.5　Dealing with profit targets

		£
	Fixed costs	25,000
add	profit target	24,000
	Contribution required	49,000

∴ must sell $\dfrac{£49,000}{£20}$ = 2,450 units

£20

In terms of value, this would be
2,450 units @ £50 unit selling price = £122,500

SELF-ASSESSMENT QUESTION 5.1

Now attempt the following self-assessment question. When you have completed it, compare your answer with the suggested solution on pages 141–143.

Heaton Postex plc

Heaton Postex plc manufactures CD players and has provided you with the following information on variable costs per unit for the current year 19–0.

Direct labour:	£20
Direct materials:	£64
Variable overheads:	£12
Total variable costs:	£96

Fixed costs: £164,000.
Selling price per unit: £120.
Expected sales: 40,000 units.

The sales target for next year, 19–1, has been set at 50,000 units, and fixed costs are expected to rise to £186,000. The selling price would rise to £125 per unit and the variable costs would increase by £4 per unit.

Calculate the following:

1. The total contribution and net profit for 19–0 and 19–1.

2. The breakeven point for 19–0 and 19–1.

3. The sales level which would have to be attained in 19–1 in order to generate a profit equal to that which was earned in 19–0.

4. The maximum amount which could be spent on additional fixed costs at a sales level of 56,000 units to produce a profit of £1,200,000.

Limiting factors

The limiting factor (also called the **key factor** or **principal budget factor**) is the factor which constrains/limits the activities of a business. Thus, when budgets are being prepared, the key factor is the starting point of the budgeting process and has to be taken into account first. For example, if sales demand was the key factor, i.e. if the company could only sell a limited number of products during a period, this would limit and determine the production needed, the amount of labour, the material requirements, and so on. It is not a sound business policy to produce more than you can sell!

Other examples of key factors are as follows:

☐ The supply of materials, e.g. Table 5.6.

☐ The availability of labour.

Table 5.6 Key factors: material supply

	Product P	Product Q
Selling price (per unit)	800	500
Variable cost (per unit)	500	300
Material required to produce one unit	4 litres	2 litres

□ Production capacity.

□ Finance.

□ Legislation.

However, key factors are not static. Management can, by its actions, eliminate them altogether or reduce their effect. What can management do where the supply of certain materials is limited? Answer: lots. Management can search for new supplies; investigate the use of a substitute; have the product redesigned to use none or less of the material concerned and to cut down on waste; improve production and inspection techniques to reduce waste and the number of defectives.

What can be done if there is a shortage of labour? Answer: quite a lot. Where labour is the key factor management can bring workers in from other areas; attract labour from other countries; introduce overtime and shift work; undertake to train or organize the training of new operatives; lease or buy labour saving machines/robots; use subcontractors.

What can management do if there is insufficient production capacity? Answer: again, quite a lot. Managers can introduce more overtime and shift work; lease or buy more machinery/robots; use subcontractors; reorganize the production flow to reduce idle/non-productive time; review the design of the product, e.g. the degree of precision needed, etc., so as to reduce the time spent making the product.

Can management do anything if finance is the key factor? Answer: yes, finance is always available from a multitude of sources, but usually at a cost which reflects the risk to the lender! In addition to loans from various sources there are also government schemes/grants; EU schemes/grants; sale and lease back; the sale of the company's own surplus fixed assets, e.g. buildings, machines, equipment and current assets, e.g. stocks of raw materials, fuels and finished goods; the issue of share capital, etc.

What can be done if the key factor is legislation? Answer: not a lot. However, management can approach local council representatives, MPs and pressure groups.

When a business's activities are constrained because of a key factor, it has to attempt to maximize its contribution. This can be done by means of a simple technique. The technique calculates *the contribution per unit of the key factor*. The alternative which gives the highest contribution per unit of the key factor, e.g. per hour or per kilo, is the one which will maximize the contribution.

EXAMPLE 5.4   Maximizing the contribution

The supply of a particular material is limited to 5,000 litres per period. It can be used to produce either product P or product Q, details of which are given in Table 5.6.

The contribution per unit of key factor, i.e. the contribution per litre, would be calculated as shown in Table 5.7.

Table 5.7 Contribution per litre

	Product P £	Product Q £
Selling price (per unit)	800	500
less Variable cost (per unit)	500	300
Contribution	300	200
$\dfrac{\text{contribution}}{\text{quantity needed}}$	$\dfrac{£300}{4}$ = **£75/litre**	$\dfrac{£200}{2}$ = **£100/litre**

The maximum contribution possible is therefore:

quantity of material available × contribution per litre

5,000 litres × £75 = £375,000
5,000 litres × £100 = £500,000

Product Q is therefore the one which should be produced. By producing it, a contribution of £500,000 is generated, £125,000 greater than the contribution which could be generated by producing product P.

 ## SELF-ASSESSMENT QUESTION 5.2

Now see if you can solve the following key factor problem; the figures do change and are more complex, but the principles/techniques remain unchanged.

Scoubado Manufacturing

Scoubado Manufacturing make three products – J, K and L. Details are given in Table 5.8.

Table 5.8 Scoubado Manufacturing: product information

	Product		
	J £	K £	L £
Selling price (per unit)	75	108	59
Cost per unit			
Direct material	30	64	20
Direct labour	6	9	4
Variable overhead	14	11	15
	50	84	39
Time taken to produce one unit	30 mins	45 mins	20 mins

The constraint under which the company is currently working is that, until management can take appropriate action, its *productive hours are limited to 42 hours per day*. However, all sales of J in excess of 30 units will have to be sold at £72 per unit; all sales of K in excess of 24 units will have to be sold at £105 per unit; and all sales of L in excess of 60 units will have to be sold at £49 per unit.

Work out the maximum contribution which could be earned per day. (For the suggested answer please turn to pages 143–144, *but only* after you have attempted to solve the problem yourself.)

The limitations and drawbacks of marginal costing

It will always be difficult to assess how both fixed costs and variable costs will be affected by changes in output. Direct labour, direct materials and variable expenses can be affected in a multitude of ways. It must be pointed out here that one of the drawbacks, which is frequently not appreciated, is that it is not always an easy task to segregate costs into their fixed and variable elements. Some items of expenditure which are very similar can be treated differently, e.g. the rent of machinery paid on a fixed rental would be treated as a fixed cost, but if the rental paid was based on output it would be treated as a variable cost! Direct labour paid a fixed amount irrespective of the level of output would be a fixed cost!

Oversimplified marginal costing can lead to the underpricing of products and a loss-making situation. The incorrect assumption made by certain users that fixed costs tend to remain constant irrespective of the level of activity, may account for the underpricing of certain products and loss-making situations.

Breakeven analysis

In Chapter 1 you were introduced to cost behaviour. However, a quick recap may prove helpful.

Fixed costs
Those costs which, in the short term, remain unchanged within a relevant range of activity (see Figure 5.2).

Variable costs
Those costs which, in the short term, vary with the level of activity within a relevant range (see Figure 5.3).

A combination of the two is known as a semi-variable or a semi-fixed cost, e.g. a cost which is made up of a fixed rental plus an amount which is paid per unit of output produced.

Figure 5.2 Fixed costs

Figure 5.3 Variable costs

At the outset you should note that breakeven analysis is a short-term planning device and should not be used in isolation but in conjunction with other data/information. You should also appreciate that in the long term there are no fixed costs. In the long term all costs are variable. However, even in the short term fixed and variable costs will only remain constant within a relevant range of output/level of activity.

The traditional breakeven chart (graph)

EXAMPLE 5.5 Constructing a breakeven chart

We will now construct a breakeven chart (pages 50–51), using the following information:

Output:	125,000 units
Sales:	£500,000
Variable cost:	£250,000
Fixed cost:	£100,000

We first draw up our chart and then insert the sales line (see Figure 5.4).

Next we draw the fixed cost line which runs parallel to the base of the chart (i.e. the output) (see Figure 5.5).

Finally, we include the variable costs by adding them on to the fixed costs. This line is drawn from £100,000 at 0 output to £350,000 at 125,000 output. This line is the total cost line, i.e. fixed cost £100,000 plus variable cost £250,000 = £350,000 total cost (see Figure 5.6).

Having completed our breakeven chart (Figure 5.6) we can read off the breakeven point at £200,000 sales and costs and 50,000 output, the point at which costs and revenue (sales/income) are equal, i.e. where the sales line crosses the total cost line.

For proof see Table 5.9 on page 51.

Figure 5.4   Sales

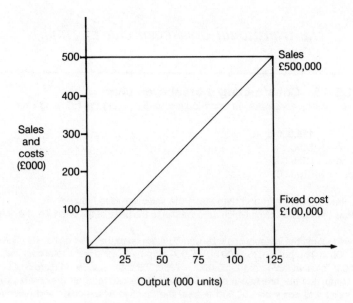

Figure 5.5   Sales and fixed costs

Figure 5.6 Breakeven point

Table 5.9 Calculating the breakeven point

		Per unit £	125,000 units £000	
	Sales	4	500	
less	Variable cost	2	250	
	Contribution	2	250	(50% profit volume ratio)
less	Fixed cost		100	
	Profit		£150	

Breakeven point = fixed cost ÷ PV ratio = £100,000 × $\dfrac{100}{50}$ = £200,000

or

= $\dfrac{\text{fixed cost}}{\text{contribution per unit}}$ = $\dfrac{£100,000}{£2}$ = 50,000 units

Now let us take a closer look at the chart which we have just completed, and see what else it can tell us (Figure 5.7).

□ The logic of the calculations involved can be followed as per the right hand side of the chart, i.e. sales £500,000 less total cost £350,000 = profit £150,000, total cost £350,000 = variable cost £250,000 + fixed cost £100,000.

□ Above the breakeven point we make a profit, below it we make a loss.

Figure 5.7 Conventional breakeven chart

☐ The margin of safety is the difference between the breakeven point and the selected output/level of activity. This indicates the extent to which the level of activity must fall before a loss-making situation is reached, and vice versa.

☐ The horizontal base line of the chart can be expressed either in terms of output or level of activity.

☐ By projecting a vertical line from the base line, e.g. at 100,000 units output (80% level of activity) we can use the chart to read off the fixed cost, total cost and sales applicable to this particular level of activity. You can see that the vertical line drawn from 100,000 units output (80% level of activity) cuts the fixed cost line at £100,000, the total cost line at £300,000 and the sales line at £400,000. The gap between sales and total cost of £100,000 represents the profit which should be achieved at the 80% level of activity: see Table 5.10 for proof.

Table 5.10 A profit proof: using marginal costing

	£000
Contribution from 100,000 units @ £2 per unit	200
less Fixed cost	100
Profit	£100

Figure 5.8 Contribution, sales and variable cost

The contribution breakeven chart (graph)

The contribution breakeven chart is an alternative way of showing the information which we used to construct our traditional breakeven chart. Using the same information as Example 5.5 we will look at its construction in two phases. Firstly, we draw up the chart and then insert the sales line and the variable cost line, both of which are drawn from the base line point 0 (see Figure 5.8).

This incomplete breakeven chart (Figure 5.8) illustrates that sales of £500,000 less variable cost £250,000 = contribution £250,000. The principal advantage of this chart is that it shows, very clearly, the contribution which is being generated at different levels of activity.

The fixed costs of £100,000 are then added to the variable costs and the total cost line drawn from £100,000 at 0% level of activity to £350,000 at 100% level of activity; the fixed costs are plotted parallel to the variable costs (see Figure 5.9).

☐ Figure 5.9 shows that below the breakeven point the fixed costs are not being covered. When the contribution generated has covered fixed costs, the remainder is profit.

☐ The final contribution breakeven chart (Figure 5.9) illustrates that the contribution, £250,000 less fixed cost £100,000 = profit £150,000.

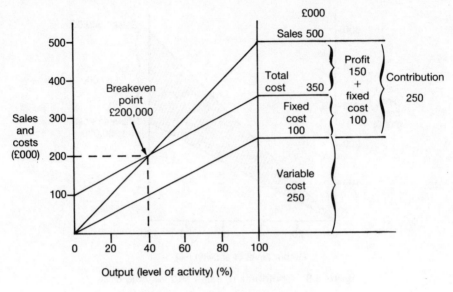

Figure 5.9 Contribution break-even chart

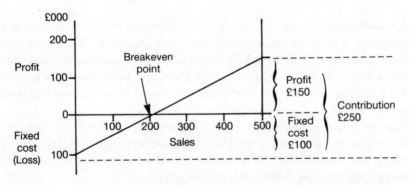

Figure 5.10 Profit graph/profit volume diagram

The profit graph/profit volume diagram

This is an alternative type of breakeven chart and should help you to understand the profit volume ratio more clearly. To draw it you need to know any two of the three figures: fixed cost, profit and breakeven point. Again, using the same figures as in Example 5.5, the graph would be as shown in Figure 5.10.

- The line which joins the fixed costs to the profit is, in fact, the contribution line, i.e. it represents fixed costs £100,000 + profit £150,000 = £250,000 contribution.
- The breakeven point is again £200,000.

 SELF-ASSESSMENT QUESTION 5.3

Now it's your turn. May I suggest that you find some graph paper and then attempt the following problem. When you have completed your answer, compare it with the suggested answer on pages 145–146.

Holme Honley Products plc

The firm's forecast figures for the forthcoming period are as shown in Table 5.11:

Table 5.11   Holme Honley Products plc forecast figures

Output (units)	25,000
	per unit
Sales	100
Variable cost	40
Fixed costs	£1,200,000

1. Prepare a breakeven chart and show the breakeven point and margin of safety.
2. Show what the position would be if the output achieved was only 15,000 units (i.e. a 60 per cent level of activity).

The limitations and drawbacks of breakeven analysis

The assumptions upon which breakeven analysis is based, e.g. how costs behave, a constant product mix, constant selling prices, etc., do not always hold true in the real world, even in the short term.

- Fixed and variable costs will not always behave as expected.
- Sales of a product may have to be made to different customers/market segments at different prices.
- The decisions made by management can affect variable and fixed costs.
- Efficiency levels within a manufacturing concern are not always constant.
- The product mix will have to respond to changes in demand and cannot therefore be forecast with accuracy.

> Sales
> less
> Variable cost
> =
> Contribution

Figure 5.11 Marginal cost equation

Remember also that the breakeven chart is most useful if used in the short term and that it should be used in conjunction with other data.

The essence

Marginal costing

Marginal costing differs from absorption costing because of the way in which it deals with fixed costs:

☐ Fixed costs, in marginal costing, are treated as **period costs**, i.e. they are written off in the period in which they are incurred.

☐ Fixed costs are not included in stock valuations and are not therefore carried forward to future accounting periods.

The marginal cost equation expresses what marginal costing is all about (see Figure 5.11). It is about the relationship between sales, variable cost and the contribution. Movements in the selling price and/or variable cost will be reflected by a corresponding movement in the contribution. If the selling price goes up or the variable cost goes down, the contribution will go up by the same amount and vice versa. The contribution generated contributes towards the recovery of fixed overheads, the remainder being the profit. The contribution per unit can be very useful when it comes to solving problems such as the following.

How many units must be sold in order to break even?

$$\frac{\text{fixed costs}}{\text{contribution per unit}} = \text{breakeven point in units}$$

How many units must be sold to produce a specified profit target?

$$\frac{\text{fixed cost} + \text{profit target}}{\text{contribution per unit}} = \text{no. of units which must be sold to achieve the profit target}$$

Note that when dealing with profit target problems, the key is to calculate the total contribution which must be generated.

The total contribution required = fixed cost + profit target.

The **profit volume ratio** explains the relationship between the contribution and sales:

$$\text{PV ratio} = \frac{\text{contribution}}{\text{sales}} \times 100 \text{ or } \frac{\text{contribution per unit}}{\text{selling price per unit}} \times 100$$

This can also be used to help solve problems, e.g. to compute the breakeven point in terms of value:

breakeven point = fixed costs ÷ PV ratio

If a constraint, e.g. the supply of materials, productive hours available, etc., limits the activities of a business, there is a **key factor (limiting factor or principal budget factor)** at work and a simple technique can be applied in order to solve the problems which emerge. The technique expresses the *contribution per unit of the key factor*, e.g. contribution per kilo, contribution per litre, contribution per hour, etc. Where a choice has to be made between alternative products, the products which give the highest contribution per unit of the key factor should be produced, as this will maximize the contribution.

The impact of a key factor can be eliminated/reduced by the actions of management.

Marginal costing, which is also called direct costing or variable costing or differential costing, is certainly a very useful decision making technique. However, it must be appreciated that its use can lead to underpricing and that it is not always as easy as might be imagined to separate fixed from variable costs.

Breakeven analysis

The construction of a breakeven chart is a relatively straightforward activity. The breakeven point can be computed mathematically, so why produce a chart? The answer lies in the fact that with the chart you can read off the position at various levels of output/activity and highlight the margin of safety. The limitations of breakeven analysis stem from the fact that in practice costs do not always behave as might be expected: sales of a product may have to be made using a variety of prices and the product mix is difficult to forecast.

Further reading

Atrill, P. and E. McLaney, *Management Accounting for Non-specialists*, Prentice Hall, 1996

Chadwick, L., *Management Accounting*, Routledge, 1993

6

Absorption costing
v. marginal costing

Objectives

When you have completed this chapter, you should be able to do the following:

- [ ] Understand why management may opt to use absorption costing or marginal costing.
- [ ] Appreciate how the two systems affect profits and stock valuations.
- [ ] Explain why, in absorption costing, there may be an under- or over-absorption (recovery) of fixed overheads.
- [ ] Understand the accounting treatment of an under- or over-absorption (recovery) of fixed overheads.
- [ ] Prepare profit statements for both methods and reconcile the profit (loss) figures revealed.

Having studied absorption (total or full) costing and marginal (variable or differential) costing, we will now look at the reasons why management may opt for one system or the other. In addition, we will show you how to prepare an absorption costing profit statement and a marginal costing profit statement and how to reconcile the two.

Absorption costing

Management adopts absorption costing in an attempt to ensure that all costs are covered. However, the drawbacks and limitations mentioned in Chapter 4 could provide good reasons for adopting the marginal costing approach. A quick recap will, perhaps, help to remind you of some of the problem areas which have to be faced when using an absorption costing system.

☐ The overheads, e.g. indirect materials, indirect labour, etc., and the direct labour hours and machine hours have to be predetermined, i.e. estimated before the commencement of the accounting period to which they relate.

☐ The bases of apportionment used to share out the overheads between user departments, e.g. floor area or number of employees, etc., and the overhead absorption (recovery) rates have to be selected, and the selection depends upon the judgement of the selector.

☐ There can be an under- or over-absorption of overheads which will have to be adjusted for at the end of the accounting period. This will be illustrated in Example 6.1, which follows shortly.

☐ The fixed costs included in the product costs are therefore carried forward to future accounting periods in the stock valuations, i.e. they are treated as unexpired costs until the goods in question are disposed of.

☐ Old and newly introduced products may both be allocated certain overhead expenditure, e.g. research and development (R&D), on an arbitrary basis when in fact all/most of it has been incurred on behalf of the newly introduced products. The effect of this is to understate the profits on the old products and to overstate the profits on the new products.

☐ There is a danger in using it for decision making because the costs it produces cannot be described as accurate. However, it is useful for the 'matching' of costs and revenues per period.

However, managers who do adopt it argue that production cannot take place without incurring certain fixed overheads (excluding selling and distribution costs) and that such costs are related to production and ought to be included in product costs, avoiding the marginal costing illusion that fixed costs have nothing to do with production.

Marginal costing

Managers who use a marginal costing approach usually accept that many overheads tend to vary more with time than output and that such costs, i.e. fixed costs, should be treated as period costs and written off in the period to which they relate. This means that fixed costs are not included in product costs and are not, therefore, carried forward to future accounting periods in stock valuations. Thus judgement about the selection of bases of

Table 6.1 Fixed costs or variable costs

Machine on	Fixed monthly rental	Rental based on production
Marginal costing treatment	Fixed OH	Variable OH
Marginal costing stock valuation	Excluded	Included

apportionment and absorption (recovery) rates, and the estimation of machine hours or direct labour hours is simply not required. There are no under- or over-recovery problems. The costs are accurate since they include only those costs, i.e. variable costs, which can be identified with and traced to the product.

However, there are difficulties and dangers in marginal costing:

□ The difficulty of classifying costs as fixed or variable (see Table 6.1).

□ The assumption by some managers that if they increase volume, profits will rise because their fixed costs will remain unchanged.

□ There are a number of limitations to the use of breakeven analysis, e.g. constant product mix, step fixed costs, etc.

However, the contribution/contribution per unit can be used to provide a lot of useful decision making information about changes in volume, changes in prices, changes in variable costs, profit targets, make or buy information, and breakeven calculations/charts.

The effects on profits and stock valuation

The following example should help you to appreciate how the two systems affect profit and stock valuations, and also how under- and over-absorptions of overheads are treated in absorption costing.

EXAMPLE 6.1   Oldwik & Co. Ltd

From the information given in Tables 6.2 and 6.3 relating to Oldwik and Co. Ltd we will now prepare two operating statements, one using the absorption costing method and the other using marginal costing.

For absorption costing purposes the fixed overheads are to be absorbed using a rate per unit of output. It is assumed that the actual variable costs and fixed costs are the same as the budget.

Answer

Before we look at anything else, we need to compute the closing stock levels in terms of units. These are quite logical calculations, and are shown in Table 6.4.

Table 6.2   Oldwik & Co. Ltd: budget for Period 1

	£	Per unit £	£	£
Sales (25,000 units)		5.20		130,000
Manufacturing cost of goods sold:*				
Variable costs	2.50		62,500	
Fixed overhead	1.10	3.60	27,500	90,000
Gross profit		1.60		40,000
less Selling and distribution expenses				18,000
Net profit				22,000

* Note: Assumes that the budgeted production will be 25,000 units (the budget for Period 2 is the same).

Table 6.3   Oldwik & Co. Ltd: actual results (units)

	Period 1	Period 2
Production	26,000	23,000
Sales	21,000	27,000

Table 6.4   Oldwik & Co. Ltd: calculating the closing stocks

	Period 1 (units)
Production	26,000
less Sales	21,000
Closing stock*	5,000
	Period 2 (units)
Opening stock (as above)	5,000
add Production	23,000
Total goods available for sale	28,000
less Sales	27,000
Closing stock	1,000

* Note: The closing stock for Period 1 becomes the opening stock for Period 2.

Absorption costing

To enable you to understand the relationship between the figures used, and to do a quick arithmetic check on the accuracy of the operating statement, you must compute the selling price/cost/gross profit per unit, as shown in Table 6.5.

Table 6.5 Oldwik & Co. Ltd: absorption costing (gross profit)

	Per unit £	Per unit £
Selling price		5.20
less Total cost:		
Variable cost	2.50	
Fixed overheads	1.10	3.60
Gross profit		1.60

The absorption (recovery) rate will work out as follows:

$$\frac{\text{budgeted fixed overheads}}{\text{budgeted production (units)}} = \frac{£27,500}{25,000 \text{ units}} = £1.10\text{p per unit}$$

i.e. for every unit produced, £1.10p is included in the costs to recover the fixed overheads.

Knowing the absorption rate and before we prepare the operating statement, we will look at both periods to see if there is any under- or over-absorption of overheads (see Table 6.6).

Table 6.6 Oldwik & Co. Ltd: under- and over-absorption of overheads

		£	
Period 1	Actual overheads	27,500	
Overheads absorbed =	Production		
	(26,000 units × £1.10)	28,600	
(exceeds the actual) =	Over-absorption	1,100	(i.e. charged too much)
		£	
Period 2		27,500	
	Actual overheads	27,500	
Overheads absorbed =	Production		
	(23,000 units × £1.10) =	25,300	
(is less than the actual) =	Under-absorption	2,200	(i.e. not enough was charged)

Now we can prepare the operating statements for Period 1 using absorption costing (Figure 6.1) and marginal costing (Figure 6.2). The reconciliation for Period 1 is given in Table 6.7 overleaf.

The difference between the two profits of £5,500 arises because in the absorption costing approach, fixed overheads at the rate of £1.10p per unit produced have been carried forward into the next accounting period via the closing stock, i.e. closing stock 5,000 units × £1.10p = £5,500 the difference between the two stock valuations (absorption costing closing stock £18,000 less the marginal costing closing stock of £12,500 = £5,500). However, this was somewhat oversimplified because there was no opening stock in Period 1.

Oldwik & Co. Ltd
  Operating statement (absorption costing) Period 1

	£	£
Sales (21,000 units @ £5.20)		109,200
less Cost of sales:		
Opening stock	Nil	
add Production: 26,000 units		
Variable cost @ £2.50	65,000	
Fixed overheads @ £1.10	28,600	
Total cost @ £3.60p	93,600	
less Closing stock (5,000 units @ £3.60)	18,000	75,600*
Gross profit (21,000 units @ £1.60)		33,600
add back Over-absorption of overheads		1,100
		34,700
less Selling and distribution expenses		18,000
Profit		£16,700

*The cost of sales figure in Period 1 represents 21,000 units @ £3.60 per unit = £75,600

Figure 6.1   Oldwik & Co. Ltd: operating statement (absorption costing)

Oldwik & Co. Ltd
  Operating statement (marginal costing) Period 1

	£	£
Sales (21,000 units @ £5.20)		109,200
less Cost of sales:		
Opening stock	Nil	
add Production 26,000 units @ £2.50)	65,000	
less Closing stock (5,000 units @ £2.50)	12,500	52,500
Contribution (21,000 units @ £2.70)		56,700
less Fixed overheads	27,500	
Selling and distribution expenses	18,000	45,500
		£11,200

*27,000 units @ £3.60 = £97,200

Figure 6.2   Oldwik & Co. Ltd: operating statement (marginal costing), Period 1

We will now look at the statements for Period 2 (Figures 6.3 and 6.4).

The reconcilation for Period 2 is given in Table 6.8 on page 66. Again, the cause of the difference is the inclusion of fixed overheads in stock valuations in the absorption costing method (see Table 6.9).

Those fixed overheads of £5,500 brought forward in the absorption cost stock valuation from Period 1 become expired costs in Period 2, i.e. they are charged as an expense because they are matched against the revenue received from their sale. This has the effect of increasing the

Table 6.7   Oldwik & Co. Ltd: profit difference
(absorption v marginal costing), Period 1

	Period 1 £
Absorption costing profit	16,700
less Marginal costing profit	11,200
	5,500

Oldwik & Co. Ltd
   Operating statement (absorption costing) Period 2

	£	£
Sales (27,000 units @ £5.20)		140,400
less Cost of sales:		
Opening stock (5,000 @ £3.60)	18,000	
add Production: 23,000 units		
Variable cost @ £2.50	57,500	
Fixed overheads @ _1.10_	25,300	
(5,000 + 23,000 units)		
= 28,000 @ £3.60	100,800	
less Closing stock (1,000 units @ £3.60)	3,600	97,200*
Gross profit (27,000 units @ £1.60)		43,200
less Under-absorption of overheads		2,200
		41,000
less Selling and distribution expenses		18,000
Profit		£23,000

Figure 6.3   Oldwik & Co. Ltd: operating statement (absorption costing), Period 2

Oldwik & Co. Ltd
   Operating statement (marginal costing) Period 2

	£	£
Sales (27,000 units @ £5.20)		140,400
less Cost of sales:		
Opening stock (5,000 units @ £2.50)	12,500	
add Production (23,000 units @ £2.50)	57,500	
= (28,000 units @ £2.50)	70,000	
less Closing stock (1,000 units @ £2.50)	2,500	67,500
Contribution (27,000 units @ £2.70)		72,900
less Fixed overheads	27,500	
Selling and distribution expenses	18,000	45,500
Profit		£27,400

Figure 6.4   Oldwik & Co. Ltd: operating statement (marginal costing), Period 2

Period 2 costs by the £5,500, but it must be remembered that this is reduced to £4,400 by the £1,100 carried forward to the next accounting period.

If the closing stock of Period 2 were sold without any further expense, the profits would be as shown in Table 6.10. If we now add all three profit figures together, the result will be as shown in Table 6.11.

The same! Why? Over a period of time, the total profits will be the same because we are dealing with the same revenues and the same costs. However, the above position, where the closing stock at the end of Period 2 is sold, will very rarely happen and was included to illustrate the point. Note that in either method we can check the gross profit or contribution figure very quickly (see Table 6.12).

Table 6.8 Oldwik & Co. Ltd: profit difference (absorption v. marginal costing), Period 2

	Period 2 £
Absorption costing profit	23,000
less Marginal costing profit	27,400
Difference	(4,400)

Table 6.9 Oldwik & Co. Ltd: reconciliation of absorption and marginal costing profits, Period 2

	Opening stocks £		Closing stocks £
Absorption costing	18,000		3,600
Marginal costing	12,500		2,500
= 5,000 × £1.10 fixed OH	5,500	= 1,000 × £1.10 fixed OH	1,100

		£
	Fixed overheads carried forward	1,100
less	Fixed overheads brought forward	5,500
	Difference	(4,400)

Table 6.10 Oldwik & Co. Ltd: profits if closing stocks are disposed of

		Absorption costing £	Marginal costing £
	Sales (1000 × £5.20)	5,200	5,200
less	Closing stock	3,600	2,500
	Profit	1,600	2,700

Table 6.11 Oldwik & Co. Ltd: total profits

	Absorption costing £	Marginal costing £
Period 1	16,700	11,200
Period 2	23,000	27,400
Sale of closing stock	1,600	2,700
Total profits	41,300	41,300

Table 6.12 Oldwik & Co. Ltd: checking gross profits and contributions

Period	Units sold	Gross profit per unit	Absorption costing gross profit	Contribution per unit	Marginal costing contribution
		£	£	£	£
1	21,000	1.60	33,600	2.70	56,700
2	27,000	1.60	43,200	2.70	72,900

 SELF-ASSESSMENT QUESTION 6.1

Oldwik & Co. Ltd

Now compare the figures produced by the two methods in the Oldwik & Co. Ltd example and explain briefly:

1. Why the under- and over-absorption of fixed overheads occurred.
2. The accounting treatment of the under- and over-absorption of the overheads.
3. The effect on profits of including fixed overheads in stock valuations as per absorption costing, when compared with marginal costing.

When you have had a go at answering these questions, compare your attempt with the suggested solution provided, which you will find on pages 146–147.

Other matters

You should also remember that the stock figures produced in the operating statements can be affected by the method of stock valuation used, e.g. average cost, first in first out (FIFO) or last in first out (LIFO), etc., which we looked at in an earlier chapter. Also, note that variations in selling prices and costs will no doubt take place and that the actual selling prices and costs are likely to differ quite significantly from those which were budgeted.

The following self-assessment question will give you a chance to see if you can prepare operating statements, using both methods and to see if you can explain the differences between the profits revealed.

 SELF-ASSESSMENT QUESTION 6.2

Kim plc

Kim plc have provided you with the information given in Table 6.13. The opening stock for the quarter of 3,000 units would be valued at £60,000 for absorption costing purposes and £45,000 for marginal costing purposes, i.e. 3,000 units @ £20 and 3,000 units @ £15 respectively. At the end of the period the actual results were as shown in Table 6.14. The actual selling prices and costs were the same as those which were budgeted.

Table 6.13   Kim plc: budget

	Per unit £	20,000 units
Direct materials and labour	12	240,000
Variable overheads	3	60,000
Marginal cost	15	300,000
Fixed cost	5	100,000
Total cost	20	400,000
Sales	24	480,000
		80,000
less Selling and distribution expenditure		29,000
Profit		51,000

Table 6.14   Kim plc: actual results (units)

Production	Sales	Closing stock
21,000	19,500	4,500

1. Prepare operating statements for the period, using:
   (a) absorption costing
   (b) marginal costing
2. Explain the difference which arises between the profits reported in the two operating statements.

When you have completed this self assessment, please turn to pages 147–150 and check your answer with the suggested answer.

The essence

Absorption costing

Companies/organizations which use absorption costing do so because they are attempting to ensure that they cover all of their production overheads (or the overheads incurred in providing a service), and also generate enough income to cover other expenses, e.g. administration, selling and distribution expenses.

Marginal costing

However, those companies/organizations which opt for marginal costing tend to do so because it is more realistic and aids the decision-making process. Marginal costing is particularly useful for illustrating what the position will be if there is change in selling prices, volume, variable costs and fixed costs. It can be used for decisions involving taking on special contracts and make or buy, etc. The costs are more accurate than those computed using absorption costing because only those costs which can be identified with or traced to the product/service are included, e.g. direct labour, direct materials and variable overheads. Marginal costing does *not* include fixed costs (costs which tend to vary more with time rather than output) in product costs and thus does not depend upon subjective judgement about methods of apportionment and the selection of absorption rates applicable to absorption costing.

The effects on profits and stock valuation

- ☐ Absorption costing includes fixed costs.
- ☐ Marginal costing excludes fixed costs.

Absorption costing stock valuations include fixed overheads via an appropriate absorption rate, e.g. per unit, per machine hour or per direct labour hour, etc. Administration, selling and distribution costs may be treated as period costs in both methods, i.e. written off, as an expense in the profit statement of the period to which they relate.

The difference between those profits (losses) computed using absorption costing and those computed using marginal costing is caused by the

Table 6.15   Reconciliation of profits/losses and closing stock valuations (Period 1)

Oldwik & Co. Ltd		Profit £	Closing stock £
Absorption costing		16,700	18,000
less Marginal costing		11,200	12,500
	Difference	5,500	5,500

Table 6.16   Reconciliation of profits/losses and stock valuations (Period 2)

Oldwik & Co. Ltd	Profit £	Opening stock b/f £	Closing stock c/f £	Net stock decrease £
Absorption costing	23,000	(18,000)	3,600	(14,400)
less Marginal costing	27,400	(12,500)	2,500	(10,000)
	(4,400)	(5,500)	1,100	(4,400)

Table 6.17   Reconciliation of profits/losses and stock
valuations (Period 2): an alternative approach

	Units	
Closing stock	1,000	carried forward (c/f)
less Opening stock	5,000	brought forward (b/f)
Net movement	(4,000)	

4,000 units × £1.10 per unit fixed overheads is equal to
the profit difference of £4,400

inclusion of fixed overheads in the absorption costing stock valuations and
their treatment in marginal costing, i.e. as period costs. In the Oldwik &
Co. Ltd example, the profits and closing stocks computed in Period 1 were
as shown in Table 6.15. The difference of £5,500 represented 5,000 closing
stock units @ £1.10p fixed cost per unit (i.e. a fixed cost per unit absorption
rate) carried forward into Period 2, to be matched against the revenue
received when it is sold. Note that there was no opening stock in Period 1.

In Period 2 the difference in profits is the net result of the fixed costs
brought forward in the opening stock and those carried forward in the
closing stock. The difference can be explained as shown in Table 6.16.

It can be observed from this illustration that the variation in profits
between the two methods will depend upon the amount which is carried
forward to the next period and the amount which is brought forward from
the last period. This can be further explained by looking at the net
movement in stock units shown in Table 6.17.

Note that over time, both methods will result in the same total profits, because they are both using the same costs and revenues.

The under- and over-absorption of overheads

In absorption costing, products are charged with fixed overheads at so much per unit, or per machine hour or per direct labour hour, i.e. using a predetermined overhead absorption (recovery rate), such as:

$$\frac{\text{budgeted fixed overheads}}{\text{budgeted units produced}} = \text{the fixed overhead rate per unit of output}$$

If the total amount of fixed overheads absorbed is greater than the actual fixed overhead expenditure there is over-absorption.

An over-absorption of fixed overheads in the profit statement should be added back to the profits (or used to reduce the loss). This is because the product costs have included too much for the overheads, which in turn reduces the gross profit calculated. If the total amount of fixed overheads absorbed is less than the actual fixed overheads incurred, this is under-absorption. An under-absorption of fixed overheads in the profit statement should be deducted from profits (or go to increase the loss), since product costs have been understated. However, note that we do not, and cannot, go back and amend product costs – they are history. A single under- or over-absorption adjustment will be done at the end of the accounting period. This is because the products/jobs are, throughout the period, accumulating a share of the overheads via the predetermined fixed overhead absorption rate.

In summary management opts for:

☐ Absorption costing in an attempt to ensure that, as far as possible all of their costs are covered.

☐ Marginal costing in an attempt to have more realistic costs which can be used for decision-making purposes.

One or the other or a combination of both can be used.

Further reading

Chadwick, L. *Management Accounting*, Routledge, 1993

7

Activity-based costing

Objectives

Having worked through the whole of this chapter, you should be able to:

☐ Describe and discuss briefly, the principal drawbacks of traditional total absorption costing.
☐ Define in your own words what is meant by:
  (a) activity-based costing;
  (b) cost objects;
  (c) resource cost drivers;
  (d) activity cost drivers;
  (e) activity cost pools.
☐ Prepare profit statements using an activity-based costing approach.
☐ Appreciate the limitations of activity-based costing.

The drawbacks of traditional total absorption costing which we reviewed in Chapter 4 provided an explanation of why it is not considered suitable for decision-making purposes. The principal drawbacks described in that chapter concerned:

☐ the problem of estimating the overheads
☐ the judgements which have to be made in connection with the allocation and apportionment to departments/cost centres
☐ the selection of the method by which service department costs are to be apportioned between user departments/cost centres
☐ the estimation of the direct labour hours and/or machine hours for use in the calculation of the absorption (recovery) rate

Figure 7.1 Activity-based costing

□ the way in which administrative expenses, selling and distribution costs, etc., are to be dealt with

□ the under- or over-absorption of fixed overheads

The principal objective of total absorption costing is to ensure that all the costs are recovered. Marginal costing which is considered more appropriate for decision-making purposes does not always lead to all of the costs being recovered. Thus, there has always been a quest for something a little more sophisticated and something which could provide management with a little more help and assistance with their product costing/decision making. Thus, in the late 1980s R. Cooper and R.S. Kaplan in the USA developed activity-based costing (ABC) a new, and more common-sense approach for assigning overheads to products, services, jobs, distribution channels, sales areas etc.

What is activity-based costing (ABC)?

A review of the definitions of activity-based costing and the diagram Figure 7.1 should provide you with a good insight into what activity-based costing is and how it works.

CIMA (Chartered Institute of Management Accountants) official terminology (1991), defines it as:

cost attribution to cost units on the basis of benefit received from indirect activities e.g. ordering, setting-up, assuring quality

It has also been defined as:

a process of using multiple cost drivers to predict and allocate costs to products and services; an accounting system collecting financial and operational data on the basis of the underlying nature and extent of business activities; an accounting information and costing system that identifies the various activities performed in an organisation, collects costs on the basis of the underlying nature and extent of those activities, and assigns costs to products and services based on consumption of those activities by products and services. (Barfield, J.T., C.A. Raiborn and M.R. Kinney, *Cost Accounting Traditions and Innovations*, West Publishing Co., 1993.)

Another definition describes it as:

the collection of financial and non-financial data about an enterprise's activities for two primary purposes:

□ Costing the enterprise's cost objectives, i.e. the products, services, batches, jobs, sales areas etc.
□ Providing information for effective cost management through activity-based management. (Burch, J.G., *Cost and Management Accounting: A Modern Approach*, West Publishing Co., 1994)

Speaking at the European Accounting Conference at Maastricht in April 1991, R.S. Kaplan said that he considered ABC to be much more than a product-costing system and that in his view it could be better described as a **resource consumption system**.

The resource costs

You need to appreciate at the outset that the costs which we are dealing with are the indirect costs, i.e. *the overheads*, as direct costs are charged direct to the cost object, e.g. the product or service. You should also note that the resource costs have still got to be estimated prior to the commencement of the budget period. The resource costs (indirect costs) could include costs such as insurance of buildings, wages and salaries, rent of premises, maintenance of equipment, depreciation of various fixed assets etc.

ACTIVITY COST POOL	ACTIVITY COST DRIVER (COST DRIVER)
Advertising	the value of sales in each sales area
Despatch	the number of despatch notes
Handling	the number of times which the material is handled
Inspection	the number of inspections
Purchasing	the number of purchase orders
Receiving (goods inwards)	the number of goods received notes
Setting-up	the number of set-ups
Stores	the number of stores issue notes

Figure 7.2 Assigning activity pool costs via activity (cost) drivers to cost objects

The ones which are specific to one cost pool can be allocated to the cost pool concerned and do not present a problem. Those which are incurred on behalf of a number of cost pools will have to be apportioned using appropriate activity cost drivers (cost drivers). The resource driver (cost driver) is linked to the usage of the resource by the activity, for example in terms of:

☐ the number of employees
☐ the area in cubic capacity
☐ hours

This type of cause-and-effect relationship is, as you may recall, used in total absorption costing. The principal difference here being that the cost centres are not production and service departments, but activities.

The activities

ABC is founded on the belief that the activities cause the costs and that the cost objects, e.g. products, services, etc., create the demand for those activities. The activities have to be identified and a cost pool (cost centre) established for each cost activity. There can be numerous activities. They can be allocated to a product/service where they are specific to that product/service. In cases where they serve a number of products/services they will have to be apportioned using activity cost drivers (cost drivers) as illustrated in Figure 7.2.

Thus, the amount assigned to each product/service will depend on the use made of the activity cost pool via an appropriate activity cost driver.

The ABC focus

ABC causes management to focus on what creates the demand for the resources and the redeployment or elimination of excess resources. ABC attempts to *estimate* the resources consumed by products.

 SELF-ASSESSMENT QUESTION 7.1

Having studied the definitions, and Figures 7.1 and 7.2, now see if you can answer the following recapitulation questions.

1 Describe briefly the principal drawbacks which are associated with total absorption costing.
2. Define activity-based costing in your own words.
3. Which two primary purposes does activity-based costing attempt to serve?
4. Give three examples of 'resource costs' and two examples of 'resource cost drivers'.
5. Give three examples of 'activity cost pools' and two examples of 'activity cost drivers'.
6. Which activity cost driver could be used for assigning costs to products/services, etc., for each of the following?
   □ advertising
   □ purchasing
   □ setting up

On completion of this self assessment, compare your answers with the appropriate sections of this chapter.
You should note that:

□ resource cost drivers attempt to measure the resources consumed by the activity cost pools, and that
□ activity cost drivers attempt to measure the activities consumed by the cost object, e.g. product, service etc. The aim is to charge the cost object with the overheads which it actually uses.

The following step-by-step Example 7.1 should help you to understand the mechanics of an activity-based costing system.

EXAMPLE 7.1

Lesaloke plc

The following indirect pre-determined resource cost categories have been identified, together with the resource cost driver by which they will be assigned to activity cost pools, for the forthcoming period:

Resource Cost	£000	Resource Cost Driver
Wages and salaries	600	Number of employees
Computing	400	Computer hours
Office space	800	Cubic capacity

The activity cost pools and data relating to their consumption of the resource costs are:

Activity cost pool	Number of employees	Computer hours	Cubic capacity
Purchasing	5	40,000	6,000
Receiving	5	4,000	18,000
Despatch	10	6,000	24,000

The activity cost pools will therefore be:

	Purchasing £000	Receiving £000	Despatch £000	Total £000
Wages and salaries	150	150	300	600
Computing	320	32	48	400
Office space	100	300	400	800
	570	482	748	1,800

The resources have now been shared out between the 'activity cost pools' according to their estimated usage of the resource costs by each of the activities, by means of the resource cost drivers.

The company sells three products N, O and P and then assigns the costs of activities to them using the following activity cost drivers:

Activity cost pool	Activity cost driver the number of
Purchasing	purchase orders
Receiving	goods received notes
Despatch	despatch notes

The following estimates have been prepared for the period:

	Products			
Number of:	N	O	P	Total
Purchase orders	5,000	2,000	600	7,600
Goods received notes	6,000	3,000	640	9,640
Despatch notes	4,000	5,000	350	9,350

From the above information we can now work out the cost per order/note for each of the activity cost drivers

	Purchasing	Receiving	Despatch
Cost	£570,000	£482,000	£748,000
Activity cost driver	7,600 orders	9,640 notes	9,350 notes
Cost per order/note	£75 per order	£50 per note	£80 per note

We can now assign the activity pool costs to the three products, as follows:

	Products			
	N	**O**	**P**	**Total**
Purchasing @ £75 per order	375	150	45	570
Receiving @ £50 per note	300	150	32	482
Despatch @£80 per note	320	400	28	748
Cost of overheads assigned to products	**995**	**700**	**105**	**1,800**

In this simplified example we only had three lots of resource costs, three activity cost pools and three products. In practice you will find that there are many more categories of resource costs, many more activity cost pools to deal with and many more products/services to contend with.

You should note that resource cost drivers and activity cost drivers can be:

□ time based

□ value based (e.g. in £s sterling)

□ transaction based

□ percentage based

The one which should be used, is the one which has a direct cause and effect relationship. Thus, with activity-based costing a choice has to be made as to which cost driver is the most appropriate for the assignment of resource costs and activity costs to cost objects.

ABC – a brief but critical evaluation

ABC seeks to find out what causes the indirect expenditure (i.e. the overheads). This is not an easy task as many of the overheads vary more with time than output and several of the suggested cost drivers are those which are already recommended for use in total absorption costing, e.g. the machine hours and the direct labour hours.

You need to note that the overheads that you are dealing with are the same overheads that you have to estimate and deal with for absorption costing purposes. You also have to select which cost driver you consider to be the most appropriate, and this is not always clear cut. In addition you have to estimate the number of machine hours, direct labour hours, set-ups, purchase orders, etc., before the period to which they relate commences.

Remember that when you deal with setting-up costs that the actual setting-up labour cost is a direct cost and should not be included in the overhead costs. For example, where a setter spends one hour setting up a machine for a production run for a batch of similar products, the setter's time can be charged to the specific batch concerned.

One recommended way of sharing out the stores cost is to use the same number of stores issue notes (stores requisitions) as the cost driver. This method does not take account of size, weight, value, handling problems, storage problems, etc. However, from this you should be able to observe and conclude that it would be impossible to find a way of sharing out this cost which could be described as both fair and accurate.

However, it is recognized that ABC is a step in the right direction, but not the end of the story, as the quest for something better continues to provoke thought, debate and research.

 SELF-ASSESSMENT QUESTION 7.2

The following self assessment assumes that you would have no problem in assigning costs to resource cost pools. The mechanics for this are very similar to those which you came across earlier in the text when you allocated and apportioned overheads to cost centres.

Pawilkes & Co. Ltd

The company manufactures two products, D and E. The following budgeted information relating to the company for the forthcoming period has been made available to you:

	Products	
	D	**E**
Sales and production (000 units)	200	200
	£	£
Selling price (per unit)	12	28
Prime cost (per unit)	8	18
	Hours	Hours
Department 1 (machine hours per unit)	.5	2
Department 2 (direct labour hours per unit)	.25	3

Details of the amounts assigned to activity cost pools and their cost drivers are:

	Activity cost pool £000	Activity cost driver
Department 1	680	Machine hours
Department 2	410	Direct labour hours
Setting up costs	40	No. of set-ups
Computing	200	No. of hours
Purchasing	100	No. of orders
	1,430	

You have also been provided with the following estimates for the period under review:

	Products		
	D (000)	**E** (000)	**Total** (000)
Machine hours	100	240	340
Direct labour hours	50	360	410
No. of set-ups	6	4	10
Computer (hours)	20	20	40
Purchasing (no. of orders)	40	10	50

Using an activity-based costing approach, prepare a profit statement which shows the profit or loss for each product and the total profit or loss.

When you have completed your attempt, compare it with the suggested solution which appears on page 150.

The essence

Traditional total absorption costing is simply an attempt to ensure that all costs are recovered. It does not produce product costs which can be described as fair and accurate and is therefore considered unsuitable for decision-making purposes.

The principal drawbacks associated with total absorption costing are:

☐ the pre-determination of overheads, and

☐ their allocation and apportionment to cost centres

☐ the estimation of figures such as machine hours and/or direct labour hours

☐ decisions regarding the treatment of administration, selling and distribution expenses

☐ the under- or over-absorption of fixed overheads

ABC (Activity-based costing)

Activity-based costing attempts to identify which of the activities cause the overhead costs and then link them up via the use of **cost drivers** (i.e. resource cost drivers and activity cost drivers) to **cost objects** such as products, services, sales areas etc. The cost objects in effect create the demand for the activities. (See Figure 7.1 for a further review of how activity-based costing systems work.) For examples of activity cost pools and activity cost drivers see Figure 7.2.

For activity-based costing to have a chance of working, it is necessary to:

☐ identify the activities

☐ create cost pools for each resource centre and each activity

☐ identify the cost drivers for resource cost drivers and activity cost drivers

☐ assign costs to cost objects, e.g. products, services etc.

It is accepted that ABC is a more accurate method for dealing with overheads than traditional total absorption costing, and a step in the right direction. However, quite a number of the recommended cost drivers are just the same as they are for total absorption costing, e.g. using the number of direct labour hours or the number of stores issue notes, and therefore suffer from the same limitations, problems and drawbacks.

Costs do not cause activities, activities cause costs.

Further reading

Atrill, P., E. McLaney, *Management Accounting for Non-specialists*, Prentice Hall, 1996
Drury, J.C., *Management and Cost Accounting*, Chapman and Hall, 1992
Horngren, C.T., *Cost Accounting*, Prentice Hall, 1996

8

Budgeting and budgetary control

Objectives

When you have reached the end of this chapter, you should:

□ Know the principles of effective budgeting.
□ Be able to explain the following terms:
  (a) a budget;
  (b) budgetary control;
  (c) the principal budget factor;
  (d) control by responsibility; and
  (e) management by exception.
□ Know why it is important to prepare a cash budget (cash flow forecast).
□ Be able to identify the differences between a cash budget and a budgeted trading and profit and loss account, and also to appreciate why the increase/decrease in the cash balance is different from the profit (loss) for a period.
□ Be able to prepare a cash budget, budgeted trading and profit and loss account and a budgeted balance sheet.
□ Appreciate that budgets are inter-related.
□ Understand how flexible budgets are constructed and why it is important to use them.
□ Be familiar with the behavioural aspects of budgeting.
□ Know how zero base budgeting (ZBB) works.

It is hoped that the unique approach taken in the introduction to this chapter will help you to understand the principles of budgeting more clearly. Together, we will take a look at the household budget and see how the principles followed there apply (even more so) to both public and private sector organizations.

Introduction: the household budget

The family depicted in our diagram (Figure 8.1) will have to do as follows:

□ Work in harmony.
□ Adopt a common-sense approach.
□ Set targets which are realistic and attainable.
□ Decide upon the allocation of its scarce resources.
□ Consider trade-offs, i.e. all of the various alternatives.
□ Appreciate the inter-relationships between the various budgets.
□ Hold meetings to discuss targets etc.
□ Set objectives.
□ Formulate policy.
□ Participate in setting budgets.
□ Co-operate, co-ordinate and communicate effectively.
□ Prepare in advance of the budget period.
□ Work to a budget preparation timetable.
□ Identify the principal budget factor (i.e. key factor or limiting factor).
□ Prepare budgets which are flexible.
□ Delegate responsibility.
□ Monitor progress.
□ Take corrective action.
□ Ensure that they take behavioural factors into account.
□ Make assumptions about the future.
□ Revise the budgets to take account of changes in the assumptions which were made.

Quite a list; but also a good indication of exactly what effective budgeting and budgetary control entails.

Principles

Having listed the principles we will now look at them in a little more depth. Managers/those responsible for the budgeting process will need to:

Figure 8.1 The household budget

□ Work together in *harmony* and *adopt a common sense approach* throughout the budgeting process. This will involve the realistic appraisal of income, expenditure and the employment of capital.

□ *Set attainable targets.* A budget which includes unattainable targets is most likely to be rejected by the personnel involved. From a management point of view, it is most important that budgets are accepted as being fair and reasonable.

□ Decide upon how they are going to *share out the scarce resources* which they have at their disposal between the competing factions, e.g. alternative projects, production needs v. research and development needs v. marketing needs and so on. This will involve discussions, negotiations, relationship skills and trade-offs.

□ Appreciate the fact that *budgets are inter-related*, e.g. there is a link between the income budget and the expenditure budget. If income is to be used for one particular type of expenditure then it is not available to finance other expenditure. (See budget relationships and Figure 8.3 later in this chapter.)

□ Attend meetings to discuss the setting of **objectives**, and the formulation of the **policy**, which they must follow in order to achieve the objectives. Many organizations do in fact have a budget committee which consists of representatives from all of the functional areas, e.g. production, marketing, finance, research and development, administration, selling and distribution, etc., and *a budget controller*, i.e. a person who oversees and co-ordinates their activities. The budget controller will seek to ensure that relevant information/data are collected, analysed, collated and distributed, to assist those who need it with their budget preparation. He/she must also attempt to secure the co-operation of others and to see that committee decisions are communicated clearly and effectively.

□ Ensure that all those who should be involved get a chance to *participate in the budget preparation process*. Participation/involvement by, e.g. certain production workers and/or supervisors can result in the setting of more realistic budgets and improved morale/motivation. The personnel involved may even bring to the attention of management, information which is vital to the success of the budgeting process.

□ Hold their meetings well before the new budget period commences. They will have to devote time to the discussion of plans, the review of data and the revision of plans, etc. Hence the need for a *timetable for the budget preparation period*, so that by the time the new budget period commences, the budget is ready to be implemented. This preparation of budgets in advance is a prerequisite for effective budgeting.

□ From the outset, *identify their principal budget factor (key factor/limiting factor)*, e.g. demand, as this will constrain their activities (see also key

Simple Budget and Actual Comparative Statement (Details of purpose, etc.) Date				
Item	Actual £000	Budget £000	Variance £000	Reasons for variance

Figure 8.2 Simple budget and actual comparative statement
Details for the previous year could also be included for comparison

factors/limiting factors in marginal costing in Chapter 5). They will also have to decide whether or not to take action designed to eliminate or reduce the effects of the principal budget factor.

□ *Plan for changes* in the basic assumptions upon which the budgets were based. This is why budgets should, where possible, be flexible, i.e. designed to change as levels of activity change, and be revised to take account of environmental change.

□ *Delegate the authority/responsibility* for a specific part of the budget to a particular person. This is known as *'control by responsibility'*. The person concerned will have to attempt, for example, to keep spending in line with the targets set and provide explanations for periods in which targets are exceeded.

□ *Monitor progress* at frequent intervals, e.g. monthly, by looking at budget and actual comparative statements, drafted along the lines of Figure 8.2.

Just like the householder, company/organization managers/executives will be particularly interested in significant adverse variances. These would be highlighted on the above type of statement/report, together with the reasons why they occurred. Managers can then devote their time and energy into putting right whatever is going wrong.

This specific attention paid to significant adverse variances is known as *management by exception*. This regular monitoring/feedback system means the early detection of items which are not going according to plan. *Early detection means early action!*

□ Appreciate that *budgets do affect people's behaviour* and that behavioural factors cannot and should not be ignored (see behavioural aspects later on in this chapter).

The variance is the difference between the actual and the budget. For example, if the actual expenditure exceeds the budgeted expenditure it is adverse, i.e. an overspend. If vice versa it would be a favourable variance.

 SELF-ASSESSMENT QUESTION 8.1

Budgetary control self check
From what you have read in this chapter so far, see if you can define, in your own words, the following key terms:

1. A budget.
2. Budgetary control.
3. The principal budget factor.
4. Control by responsibility.
5. Management by exception.

When you have attempted to answer this self-assessment question, please turn to pages 151–153 to compare your answer with that suggested.

Practical considerations

Having established the principles of budgeting and budgetary control, we will conclude this section of the chapter by pointing out a number of practical considerations.

Firstly, there needs to be an acceptance throughout the company/organization that budgeting is *a management planning technique* and that its use can greatly improve efficiency. Yes, budgeting/budgetary control should help the company/organization to compete in the market place and promote its long-term survival. Managers should therefore show by their actions that they accept and approve of the budget. Their *acceptance/approval* should be very clearly communicated to all those concerned. They should ensure that all of the personnel involved in the budgeting process are *educated* as to its benefits/principles and the way in which it operates within the company/organization.

A minor point, worthy of note, is that the actual and budgeted figures must match as regards content, i.e. they must be computed in the same way.

Finally, control should really be directed towards problem solving, constructive comments and the taking of corrective action by management rather than recrimination.

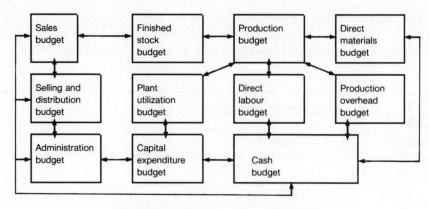

Figure 8.3   Budget inter-relationships

Budget relationships

The budgeting process is rather like a large jigsaw, i.e. all the pieces must fit together, because together they should form a coherent picture (see Figure 8.3). Budgets are interrelated. Something which affects one budget will tend to have a ripple effect in that it will also affect other budgets. Thus during the budget preparation period the budget committee has to meet regularly to ensure that the individual functional budgets, e.g. sales, production, plant utilization, etc., all match up.

EXAMPLE 8.1   The calculation of budgeted production
Data relating to the forthcoming budget period are shown in Table 8.1.
   The budgeted closing stock position dictates that a further 800 units be produced. This means that the production budget would be as in Table 8.2.

Table 8.1   Calculation of budgeted production to satisfy the sales budget

	Budget (units)
Opening stock of finished goods	500
Closing stock of finished goods	800
Sales	12,400
To satisfy sales would need:	
Opening stock	500
Production	11,900
	12,400

Table 8.2 The production budget

	Units
Made to resell	11,900
Made for stock	800
Production budget	12,700

The 12,700 units could be produced provided the company/organization had sufficient plant capacity, could organize an adequate supply of direct materials and direct labour, and had enough finance available. Thus, if the sales budget, which in the absence of a principal budget factor is the most usual starting point, is increased, the production budget will also have to be increased, as will the direct material budget and so on.

The cash budget

The diagram about budget inter-relationships, Figure 8.3, which we have just looked at, clearly illustrates that the cash budget (also called a cash flow forecast) interacts with numerous other budgets. A common cause of business failure has been identified as poor cash flow management. The cash budget is a very important and integral part of good cash flow management. Cash budgeting aims to do the following:

□ Make sure that cash is available when it is needed.

□ Identify shortages in good time, so that appropriate remedial action can be taken.

□ Identify surpluses of cash, so that where possible they can be transferred/invested where they can earn a satisfactory return. Nowadays, the treasury function of a company/organization deals with the investment of surplus cash in the short term, e.g. overnight or for, say, a week or a month.

The cash budget is drawn up using predetermined figures. It records them during the month in which they are expected to come in or go out. In doing this it has to take periods of credit allowed by suppliers or to customers into account. So, for example, it does not really matter about the month in which a sale is made or the period covered by a dividend received. What does matter is when the cash from the sale or the dividend is actually received. Thus, non-cash items, e.g. depreciation, are not included in the cash budget. The cash moves when the asset is paid for not when it is depreciated.

We will now take you through a step-by-step example, which will show you how the cash budget is prepared.

EXAMPLE 8.2   A cash budget

Brendug and Co. Ltd

1. First of all we have to estimate the cash flows for the forthcoming period, taking into account past performance, future plans and relevant data. Let us assume that this has now been done for Brendug and Co. Ltd and the information generated is as given in Table 8.3.

2. Insert the opening balance for the period. (Our example is a start up situation, so this does not apply.)

3. Fill in the above information vertically, column by column, taking into account the periods of credit. The cash budget will then appear as shown in Table 8.4, for the period of six months to 30 June 19–3.

4. Add up the January inflows and subtract the January outflows to calculate the closing balance, as in Table 8.5.

The closing balance of £37,000 for January is then carried down as the opening balance for February; to this will be added any February inflows and the February outflows will be deducted, as shown in Table 8.6.

This process will be repeated until the closing balance for June has been computed. When it has, the cash budget will then look like Table 8.7.

5. Having worked out the June closing balance of £24,000, we can then add up each column (other than the opening and closing balance columns) as indicated above. Why?

Table 8.3   Brendug and Co. Ltd: cash budget data

19–3	
January	During this month the company planned to commence trading and receive cash of £100,000 from an issue of £1 ordinary shares.
January	To pay £48,000 for plant and machinery. This will be depreciated at 10% of cost per annum.
January	To pay a half year's rent in advance of £12,000.

Sales would be £8,000 in January and then £16,000 per month thereafter. Customers (i.e. debtors) would be given *two months' credit*.

Purchases of raw materials would be £6,000 in January and then £12,000 per month thereafter. Suppliers (i.e. creditors) will only allow *one month's credit*.

Wages and general expenses have been estimated to be £3,000 per month payable during the month in which they are incurred.

The budgeted closing stock of raw materials is £6,000.

Although this is not part of the cash budget, we can then use this information together with the outstanding debtors and creditors to produce a budgeted trading and profit and loss account and balance sheet. This will help you understand:

☐ The difference between a cash budget and a budgeted trading and profit and loss account.

☐ The difference between profit and cash.

Table 8.4 Brendug and Co. Ltd: cash budget (1) (£000)

| | Inflows | | | Outflows | | | |
	Opening balance	Share capital	Sales	Purchases	Rent	Wages & general expenses	Fixed assets	Closing balance
Jan	–	100	–	–	12	3	48	
Feb		–	–	6	–	3	–	
Mar		–	8	12	–	3	–	
Apr		–	16	12	–	3	–	
May		–	16	12	–	3	–	
Jun		–	16	12	–	3	–	

Table 8.5 Brendug and Co. Ltd: calculating
the closing balance for January

		£000
	Inflows	100
less	Outflows (12 + 3 + 48)	63
	= Closing balance	37

Table 8.6 Brendug and Co. Ltd: calculating
the closing balance for February

		£
	Opening balance + inflows	37
less	Outflows	9
		28

Notice that we did not use the closing stock of raw materials or deal with any depreciation in the cash budget.

The budgeted trading and profit and loss account and the budgeted balance sheet

We adjust the totals for the cash budget (step 5 in Example 8.1) to provide the figures which we need to produce the budgeted trading and profit and loss account and balance sheet, as shown in Table 8.8.

Taking into account the closing stock of £6,000 and depreciation of £2,400 (£48,000 × 10% for half a year) we can now draft the budgeted trading and profit and loss account, as shown in Table 8.9.

Finally, we can list all of the budgeted balances as at 30 June 19–3 to produce the budgeted balance sheet (see Table 8.10).

The master budget

You should note that the cash budget, budgeted trading and profit and loss account, and the budgeted balance sheet are frequently referred to as the **master budget**. If management approves it, it will be implemented. If it is not approved, than it is back to the drawing board to review and revise targets, policies, etc. The master budget, once approved, is the culmination of the budget preparation process.

Table 8.7 Brendug and Co. Ltd: cash budget (2) (£000)

| | Inflows | | | Outflows | | | | |
	Opening balance	Share capital	Sales	Purchases	Rent	Wages & general expenses	Fixed assets	Closing balance
Jan	–	100	–	–	12	3	48	37
Feb	37		–	6	–	3	–	28
Mar	28		8	12	–	3	–	21
Apr	21		16	12	–	3	–	22
May	22		16	12	–	3	–	23
Jun	23		16	12	–	3	–	24
(Step 5)		100	56	54	12	18	48	

Table 8.8   Brendug and Co. Ltd: converting cash budget information into a budgeted trading, profit and loss account and balance sheet (£000)

Share capital	Sales		Purchases	Rent	Wages & general expenses	Fixed assets
<u>100</u>	56		54	12	18	48
Debtors (2 mth × £16)	<u>32</u> <u>88</u>	Creditors (1 mth × £12)	<u>12</u> <u>66</u>			

Table 8.9   Brendug and Co. Ltd: budgeted trading and profit and loss account

		£000	£000
	Sales (£56 received in cash + £32 owing from customers)		88
less	Cost of Sales		
	Opening stock	–	
add	Purchases (£54 in cash + £12 owing to suppliers)	<u>66</u>	
		66	
less	Closing stock	<u>6</u>	<u>60</u>
	Gross profit		28
less	Expenses:		
	Rent	12	
	Wages and general expenses	18	
	Depreciation of plant and machinery	<u>2.4</u>	<u>32.4</u>
	Net profit (Loss)		<u>(4.4)</u>

Table 8.10   Brendug and Co. Ltd: budgeted balance sheet

		£000	£000
CAPITAL EMPLOYED			
	Share capital	100	
Reserves			
	Retained profits (loss)	<u>(4.4)</u>	<u>95.6</u>
EMPLOYMENT OF CAPITAL			
Fixed assets:			
	Plants and machinery	48	
less	Depreciation	<u>2.4</u>	45.6
Working capital			
Current assets:			
	Stock	6	
	Debtors (2 months × £16)	32	
	Cash and bank (per cash budget)	<u>24</u>	
		62	
less	**Current liabilities**		
	Creditors (1 month × £12)	12	<u>50</u> <u>95.6</u>

SELF-ASSESSMENT QUESTION 8.2

The difference between profit and cash

Now compare the cash budget in Table 8.7 (Example 8.2), with the budgeted trading and profit and loss account of Brendug and Co. Ltd and explain why the cash balance of £24,000 differs from the loss of £4,400. You will find the answer to this assessment on pages 153–154.

SELF-ASSESSMENT QUESTION 8.3

Having completed the above self assessment question now see if you can prepare a cash budget, budgeted trading and profit and loss account and balance sheet on the worksheets provided for Jeanles Ltd.

Jeanles Ltd

Jeanles Ltd are to commence trading in a few months' time on 1 January 19–4 with cash from issued share capital of £60,000. They have provided you with information relating to their first six months (Table 8.11).

Using the worksheets and the data provided, prepare a cash budget for the half-year to 30 June 19–4 (Table 8.12), a budgeted trading and profit and loss account for the half-year (Table 8.13), and a budgeted balance sheet (Table 8.14) as at 30 June 19–4.

You will find the suggested answer on pages 154–156.

Flexible budgets

A company/organization can either use a fixed budget or a flexible budget. A fixed budget is a budget which is designed to remain unchanged irrespective of the level of activity (i.e. level of output) actually attained, whereas a flexible budget is a budget which, by recognizing the differences between fixed, semi-fixed and variable costs, is designed to change in relation to the level of activity attained. An example of a flexible budget is shown in Table 8.15.

A fixed budget is not really suitable for comparing performance because you could be comparing two completely different levels of activity. The idea behind flexible budgeting is to overcome that problem so that the actual level of activity attained can be compared with a budget appertaining to the same level of activity.

Table 8.11 Jeanles Ltd: cash budget data

	£	
Quarterly rent of premises, payment due in January and April	1,400	(per quarter)
Cash outlay on equipment – payable January	59,000	
payable March	16,000	
Monthly planned purchase of stock for resale		
January	10,000	
February	15,000	
March to June (per month)	21,000	
All stock is bought on two months' credit (i.e. January purchases are paid for in March)		
Monthly planned sales are		
January	8,000	
February	20,000	
March–June (per month)	28,000	

All sales are on one month's credit. No bad debts or arrears of payments are expected. The budgeted closing stock for 30 June 19–4 should be £4,000.

The monthly cash outlay on general expenses is expected to be £500, and wages and salaries are expected to be £1,000 per month. Depreciation of equipment is to be at 20% of cost per annum. The agreed overdraft limit is £7,500.

EXAMPLE 8.3 Fixflex plc

We have been supplied with the information given in Table 8.16. If we compare these figures we will see that a significant proportion of the variances is a direct result of comparing two different levels of activity, i.e. a budget of 30,000 units with an actual performance of 25,000 units.

Taking cost behaviour into account we can recompute (i.e. *flex*) the budget to the actual level achieved and this will provide us with a more realistic and valid comparison, as given in Table 8.17.

The aim of this section is for you to appreciate how flexible budgets are constructed and understand why a business/organization should use them. It is not the intention that you should become proficient in the 'number crunching' aspect of flexible budgeting.

The behavioural aspects of budgeting

Budgeting takes place within a human environment and behavioural factors cannot be pushed aside and ignored. Budgets are in fact designed to affect people's behaviour. However, people do not always respond as

Table 8.12 Cash budget: work sheet

	Inflows		Outflows					
	Opening balance	Sales	Purchases	Rent	Wages & Salaries	General expenses	Fixed assets	Closing balance
Jan								
Feb								
Mar								
Apr								
May								
Jun								

Table 8.13 Budgeted trading and profit and loss account: work sheet

		£	£
	Sales		
less	Cost of sales		
	Opening stock		
add	Purchases	―――	
less	Closing stock	―――	―――
	Gross profit		
less	Expenses		
	Rent		
	Wages & salaries		
	General expenses		
less	Depreciation	―――	―――
	Net profit (Loss)		―――

expected. Their response could be affected by the way in which the budget was drawn up; their involvement/lack of involvement in the preparation of the budget; the way in which it was communicated; their education and training; the way in which the budget is to be implemented and so on. Some of the causes of the behavioural problems relating to budgeting, which are frequently encountered in a company/organization are listed overleaf:

Table 8.14 Budgeted balance sheet: work sheet

	£	£
CAPITAL EMPLOYED		
Issued ordinary share capital		
Retained profit	_____	_____
EMPLOYMENT OF CAPITAL		
Fixed assets		
less Depreciation	_____	
Working capital		
Current assets		
Stock		
Debtors		
Cash and bank	_____	
less **Current liabilities**		
Creditors		
Bank overdraft	_____	_____

Table 8.15 Monthly departmental flexible budget

	£000	£000	£000	£000	£000	
Sales	80	90	100	110	120	
Direct costs						
(e.g. finished goods, wages)	24	27	30	33	36	
Variable overheads	8	9	10	11	12	
Semi-fixed overheads	5	6	7	8	9	
Fixed overheads	15	15	15	15	17	(step)
	52	57	62	67	74	
Profit	28	33	38	43	46	

☐ *Perceptions*

Perceptions about the objectives of a company/organization and the interpretation of policy. This is caused by poor communications and a lack of participation.

☐ *Personal goals*

Those who have to abide by the budget and achieve the targets set, also have their own personal objectives. These personal objectives may conflict and run counter to the objectives laid down by management. For

Table 8.16 Fixflex plc: budget/actual information

	Budget August 19–4	Actual August 19–4
Production (units)	30,000	25,000
	£	£
Labour – variable	36,000	33,000
Variable overheads	4,500	3,625
Fixed overheads	5,400	5,400

example, departmental heads may become too preoccupied with their own advancement and empire building, at the expense of achieving budget targets.

□ *Participation*
A principle of budgeting which is sometimes overlooked, results in those who should be involved and consulted deciding to withdraw their full-hearted co-operation and support. They may even fail to point out something to management which could well have saved a lot of money and a great amount of time dealing with unnecessary problems.

□ *Aspiration levels*
The achievement of the budget is perceived or treated as success and non-achievement perceived or treated as failure. This can affect *motivation and morale*.

□ *Targets*
If targets are set too high employees may opt out of trying to achieve them. However, if they are set too low, e.g. in an incentive scheme, employees may agree between themselves what the level of production should be! This is because they are afraid that targets will be revised if managers realize they have set the targets too low.

□ *Obsession*
Some managers are obsessed by the idea that the budget must be achieved at all costs. This is partly due to their aspirations and an uncalled-for perception of accuracy. Some managers tend to forget that the budgeted figures are only estimates.

□ *An excuse*
If things do go wrong, e.g. where there are organizational problems, it is not uncommon for the budget to get the blame. And if some managers/supervisors wish to justify something which has to be done, they say 'Oh well, we have to do this to keep within our budget'. This then leads their subordinates to treat the budget as a whipping post.

□ *Resource allocation*
This is always an area in which conflict can arise, possibly as a result of departmental goals/empire building.

Table 8.17 Fixflex plc: budget/actual comparative statement

	Budget August 19–4 Per unit £	Budget August 19–4 25,000 units £	Actual August 19–4 25,000 units £	Variance £
Labour $\frac{(£36,000)}{(30,000)}$	1.20	30,000	33,000	(3,000)
Variable overheads $\frac{(£4,500)}{(30,000)}$	0.15	3,750	3,625	125
Fixed overheads	—	5,400	5,400	—
		39,150	42,025	2,875

Note: The fixed costs are assumed to remain unchanged in this example.

☐ *Imposition*
If management imposes budgets, 'from above', the personnel who 'work below' may reject them and fail to pledge their support or generally just show a lack of enthusiasm.

☐ *Sub-optimal decisions*
If budgets have to be cut, an across-the-board cut will weaken both the strong and the weak! Again, this will undoubtedly result in conflict.

Management therefore needs to tread very carefully when preparing and introducing budgets. To some extent success will depend upon the way in which managers deal with the education and training of their employees, employee participation, good clear communications and the regular review and monitoring of behavioural factors.

The benefits of budgeting

Effective budgeting improves efficiency in that it demands the following:

☐ Careful planning and the provision of information/data for management.

☐ The participation of both management and workers.

☐ Co-ordination and co-operation.

☐ A sound accounting system.

☐ That new trends and inefficiencies are detected at an early stage of the planning/control process.

☐ The delegation of duties/authority. This will mean that job specifications will have to be clear and unambiguous.

☐ Control by responsibility.

☐ Management by exception.

☐ A sound evaluation system for comparing/reporting on budgeted and actual results.

☐ The motivation of the work force.

☐ Good clear communications.

☐ Corrective action by management to remedy adverse situations.

This can happen only if all those who are involved understand what budgeting is trying to do and are able to express their views during the budget preparation process, and if the budget is flexible enough to take account of changes in circumstances.

Zero base budgeting

Another approach to budgeting is that of zero base budgeting (ZBB). This has been found to be particularly useful in service/support areas, e.g. canteen, welfare, research and development. It forces the managers who are responsible for budgets to justify them and to rank them according to their importance, and also to evaluate more/less costly alternatives. Top management can then screen and discuss the proposals and decide which ones will go ahead. This, it is claimed, promotes a much more efficient allocation of resources. This is because managers have to justify the following:

☐ How much they want.
☐ Why they want it.
☐ How else they could achieve the same result.
☐ The degree of importance which they attach to it.

The essence

Managerial aspects

Budgeting is a management technique. Management needs to set objectives and formulate policy. The budgets provide targets which reflect the objectives, and the policy is the means by which those targets should be achieved. Management must see that the targets which are set are fair, reasonable and attainable. To produce effective budgets managers must do the following:

☐ Secure the co-operation and participation of employees, e.g. supervisors, and certain shop floor workers.
☐ Communicate clearly and indicate acceptance of the budget.
☐ Possess negotiation/relationship skills and be able to cope with behavioural problems.
☐ Delegate the authority and responsibility for budgets to subordinates.
☐ Plan the budget preparation process well in advance of the forthcoming budget period, e.g. timetables for meetings, etc. The aim is to ensure that the budget is ready to be implemented before the start of the new budget period.
☐ Host/attend the appropriate meetings at which their own budget/certain other budgets will be reviewed/discussed.

- ☐ Appoint a person to act as budget controller.
- ☐ Set up an effective monitoring and reporting system to compare budgeted with actual results at frequent intervals.
- ☐ Be prepared to take action to put right something which is going wrong, as indicated by the feedback from comparative statements/reports.

Budget preparation

It is essential that the budget preparation process commences well before the budget period to which it relates and that the principal budget factor (i.e. a constraint) is identified. The preparation process will be co-ordinated by the budget controller. The authority and responsibility for a particular budget/section of a budget will be delegated to a named individual. The budget controller will supply that person with appropriate information/ data to help with their budget preparation. From the outset all those involved will have to be issued with instructions and a timetable. The timetable will state when schedules and other information will be required and the dates and times of meetings. Meetings are needed to plan, discuss, review and revise the budgets, to ensure that everything fits together. This is because budgets are interrelated. One budget cannot be prepared in isolation and without reference to the other budgets. When the process is complete, managers must ensure that the information on objectives, policy, targets, etc., is communicated to the appropriate personnel, which indicates managers' acceptance of the budget.

Budgetary control

Control in budgeting is exercised by regular comparisons (e.g. monthly) between budgeted and actual results. The statements/reports produced inform management of where, in their company/organization things are not going according to plan. Management can then decide on the form of corrective action which needs to be taken (see Figure 8.4).

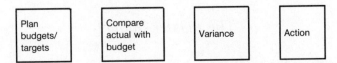

Figure 8.4 Budgetary control

Cost control

Management will be particularly interested in the significant adverse variances which will be highlighted in statements and reports. This system, which singles out those variances which management should look at very carefully, is known as *management by exception*. Managers spend their time and energy putting right things which are going wrong and keeping the company/organization on course to achieve its objectives. Frequent comparisons do provide an early warning system/early detection system of inefficiencies, the emergence of new trends and environmental changes.

Control is also exercised by delegating to an individual the responsibility for a particular budget or subsection of a budget, i.e. *control by responsibility*. That person alone has to justify and explain to management why targets have not been achieved.

However, if the reported variances are to be any use it is essential that the budgeted and actual figures have been computed the same way and relate to the same level of activity. This is why if at all possible a flexible budget should be used, i.e. a budget which is designed to change as the level of activity changes.

Finally, remember that control should be directed towards problem solving and not the creation of conflict!

More effective budgeting

If budgeting is to become really effective it must be remembered that it is only a forecast. The budget itself, once implemented, must be monitored at frequent intervals, and if necessary amended to take account of changes in the basic assumptions upon which it was based.

Management will also have to monitor *behavioural factors* on a regular basis. People problems, if allowed to fester and multiply, can become the principal reason for the non-attainment of budget targets.

Staff education can be a most worthwhile investment. If staff know more about budgeting and what it is trying to do, then provided that they are able to *participate*, and express their opinions, more reasonable, accurate and realistic budgets should be produced.

The master budget

This consists of the following:
□ A cash budget.

□ A budgeted trading and profit and loss account.
□ A budgeted balance sheet.

It is the coming together of all the component parts of the budgeting jigsaw. It communicates in advance of the budget period commencing (e.g. a six- or twelve-month period) the outcome in terms of cash flow, profits, assets and liabilities, etc.

Zero base budgeting

This provides a system of ranking budget packages according to their importance and is suitable for services/non-profit making activities.

Further reading

Chadwick, L., *Management Accounting*, Routledge, 1993
Harper, W.M., *Cost and Management Accounting*, Pitman, 1995

9

Standard costing

Objectives

When you have worked through this chapter you should be able to:

☐ Understand what a standard is, and some of the considerations involved in its composition.

☐ Appreciate that a cost variance can be subdivided into a price variance and a quantity variance.

☐ Understand why a variance is either adverse or favourable.

☐ Appreciate the kind of information which should be given in variance analysis reports and statements.

☐ Compute simple labour and material variances.

☐ Define some of the variances in your own words.

☐ Know some of the causes of labour variances and material variances.

☐ Understand how it is possible to reconcile the standard profit with the actual profit.

However, please note it is not the intention of this chapter that you become an expert in dealing with the numbers involved. The principal aims are simply that you should be able to follow the workings and understand the principles involved.

What are standard costs?

A standard cost is a predetermined target cost designed to provide a yardstick against which to measure actual performance. The setting of a

Figure 9.1 Variance analysis

standard may involve consideration of quantities, prices, rates of pay, qualities and a detailed review of all the relevant factors. Standards can be set for selling prices and the elements of cost, i.e. materials, labour and overheads.

Cost control using standard costing

Control in standard costing is achieved by variance analysis. Figure 9.1 should help you to understand how variance analysis works. At the end of the period under review the actual cost is compared with the predetermined standard cost for the actual level of activity which was attained. This difference is known as the total or cost variance. All variances are the result of two factors, price and quantity. Thus, the total or cost variance can be subdivided into that part of the variance which arises from price differences and that part which arises from differences in quantities. The names of these subvariances may cause confusion, but the principles remain unchanged. Table 9.1 should make the position a little clearer.

Variance analysis – reports and statements

The reports and statements should be presented to management at frequent intervals and indicate which variances are:

☐ *Adverse (or negative)*: e.g. spending more than planned.
☐ *Favourable (or positive)*: e.g. spending less than planned.

Table 9.1   Variances: materials, labour, overheads and sales

	Total/cost variance	Price variance	Quantity variance
Materials	Material cost variance	Material price variance	Material usage variance
Labour	Labour cost variance	Labour rate variance	Labour efficiency variance
Overheads	Overhead cost variance	Overhead expenditure variance	Overhead volume or efficiency variance
Sales	Sales margin variance	Sales margin price variance	Sales margin volume variance

Table 9.2   Control by responsibility: variance analysis

Variance	Responsible person
Labour efficiency variance	Production manager or Departmental manager or Foreman
Material price variance	Chief buyer

If at all possible, they should also distinguish between those variances which are controllable, i.e. those which management can do something about, and those variances which are uncontrollable, i.e. where management can do nothing or very little. In practice, management does tend to have more control over quantity variances and less control over price variances.

The reports/statements should also attempt to:

☐ Highlight significant controllable adverse variances.

☐ Inform management of the reasons why certain variances have occurred.

The highlighting of variances is an example of management by exception. Managers can devote themselves towards resolving the problems identified. They can focus their time, attention and expertise on deciding the form of any corrective action which needs to be taken.

The operation of a control by responsibility policy is another important part of the process. Specific members of the work force will need to take on the responsibility for particular variances (see Table 9.2).

Material variances

To illustrate the numbers side of standard costing and to continue what is intended to be a gentle introduction to the subject, we will now take a look at an example. We will work out the figures and then take a step back and look carefully at what they actually mean.

EXAMPLE 9.1   Material variances

The standard cost of material used for the budget of 10,000 units of product K, for Period 3, 19–2 was:

30,000 kilos (i.e. 3 kilos per unit) @ £2 per kilo = £60,000

Actual production of product K for Period 3, 19–2 was:

8,000 units which took 26,000 kilos of material at a cost of £1.85 per kilo = £48,100

Answer

The first thing which you should note is that the budgeted level of activity (i.e. production output) is 10,000 units and the actual level of activity is 8,000 units. To compare our actual costs for 8,000 units with the standard for 10,000 units is incorrect. Why? Because we need to compare the standard and actual costs for the same level of activity: we need to compare like with like. Thus we need to calculate the standard cost for the actual level of activity and use that in our calculations, as follows:

8,000 units × 3 kilos per unit = 24,000 kilos @ £2 = £48,000

The second point which you need to note is that the actual price paid of £1.85 for the material is 15p per kilo less than the standard price of £2. Thus, you know from the outset that your price variance is going to be favourable. From this information you can see that the actual material used of 26,000 kilos is greater than the standard, i.e. the planned, use of materials 24,000 kilos, by 2,000 kilos. Using more material than planned in this way is called an adverse material usage variance.

For the calculations see Table 9.3 and for the proof see Figure 9.2, overleaf.

 SELF-ASSESSMENT QUESTION 9.1

By looking at the above calculations, see if you can define in your own words, what is meant by:

1. The material cost variance.
2. The material price variance.
3. The material usage variance.

When you have completed your attempt, compare your answer with the suggested answer on pages 154–157.

Table 9.3   Material variances

	Material cost variance £	Material price variance £	Material usage variance £
Actual material used at actual price (26,000 kilos @ £1.85)	48,100	48,100	
Standard material used (for actual level of activity) at standard price (24,000 kilos @ £2)	48,000		48,000
Actual material used at standard price (26,000 kilos @ £2)		52,000	52,000
	100	3,900	4,000
	(adverse)	(favourable)	(adverse)

Figure 9.2   Material variances

What factors will be taken into account when computing the standard material cost? The determination of the standard material cost involves:

☐ *Material quantities (material utilization)*
You will need to consider maximum economies in material usage (assisted by the designers and other appropriate personnel); the setting of standard sizes and standard losses; waste, etc.

☐ *Material prices*
You will need to consider the efficiency of store-keeping and purchasing; forecasts of average prices of materials for future periods allowing for discounts, carriage and handling charges; information and advice from the purchasing department; and the analysis of trends.

☐ *Quality*
You will need to pay attention to design department recommendations/ stipulations; appearance, strength; quality policy; range of materials

available; setting of machines and equipment; material specifications; the question of whether to make or buy the components, etc.

The calculation of the sub-variances

Managers, executives and students frequently ask for an explanation as to why we calculate the sub-variances in the following way:

Price variance
Actual Price less (Standard Price × Actual Quantity)
or
(Actual Price × Actual Quantity) less (Standard Price × Actual Quantity)

Quantity variance
Actual Quantity less (Standard Quantity* × Standard Price)
or
(Actual Quantity × Standard Price) less (Standard Quantity* × Standard Price)

This is best explained by reviewing Figure 9.3 from which you can clearly observe the two sub-variances and the way in which they are calculated. Remember also, that the two sub-variances when added together should add up to the total (cost) variance that has been arrived at by comparing:

(Actual Price × Actual Quantity) less (Standard Price × Standard Quantity*)

*This should be the standard quantity for the actual level of activity (output).

Figure 9.3 The sub-variances

Figure 9.4   Material mix and yield variances

Other material variances

It should be remembered that the material usage variance can, where appropriate, be subdivided further into a mix variance and a yield variance (see Figure 9.4), e.g. in the chemicals industry. This will involve sorting out a standard recipe which stipulates the quantities of each material required and the assessment of a standard yield which takes into account anticipated processing losses.

What can cause a materials price variance? Some of the reasons for a materials price variance are:

☐ Supplier's price change/using a new supplier.

☐ Loss/reduction of trade discount.

☐ Purchase of a different quality from that which was planned.

What can cause a material usage variance?

☐ The quality of the material being used, different from that which was planned.

☐ Pilferage.

☐ Inefficient production workers/methods.

☐ Using unskilled workers to do skilled work.

Labour variances

We will now take a look at labour variances by working through the following self assessment.

 SELF-ASSESSMENT QUESTION 9.2

Using the following information, see if you can complete the variance calculations on the work sheet provided (Figure 9.5).

☐ Standard labour rate: £8.

☐ Hours: 2 hours per component.

WORK SHEET

Standard costing
labour variances

	Labour cost variance £	Labour rate variance £	Labour efficiency variance £
Actual hours @ actual rate	☐	☐	
Standard hours @ standard rate for actual level of activity	☐		☐
Actual hours @ standard rate		☐	☐
	£ ———	£ ———	£ ———

(State whether it is adverse or favourable)

Summary (proof) £

Labour rate variance
Labour efficiency variance
= **labour cost variance** ———

Figure 9.5 Standard costing labour variances

The following are actual production data:

☐ 1,000 components produced.
☐ Labour rate: £8.50.
☐ 1,950 hours worked.

Now check your answer, with the suggested answer/additional notes on pages 157–158.

What factors will need to be taken into account when calculating the standard cost of labour? The calculation of the standard cost of labour involves a thorough analysis of operations, and possibly a grading review. In order to ascertain the standard labour costs it is necessary to decide upon:

☐ *Labour quantities*
The setting of standard times may be by:

(a) using past performance records, e.g. the payroll analysis.

(b) test runs/work study allowing for fatigue and unavoidable losses.

Standard times are to be set for each grade of labour for each cost centre/department.

☐ *Labour rate standard and grades of labour*
Analysis of all factors likely to affect wage rates will help to foretell the actual rate which should be paid during the next period, e.g. a year. The personnel department should be able to provide most of the information. Other factors such as bonus payments, piece rates, overtime premiums, etc., will have to be taken into account.

☐ *Labour grades*
Skills required and operations involved, volume of work, division and availability of labour, should all be considered. The work study and personnel departments should combine to provide these data. Other factors such as sex, age, apprenticeship details, etc., should also be reviewed.

Labour rate variances may be caused by the following:

☐ A rate increase, different from that which was anticipated.

☐ Using a different grade of worker, e.g. using a skilled worker to do a semi-skilled operation.

☐ Overtime/bonus and shiftwork payments.

The causes of a labour efficiency variance could be as follows:

☐ Idle (non-productive) time, e.g. training a new operative resulting in lower productivity, machine breakdown, waiting for work or materials, etc.

☐ Poor working conditions, e.g. too hot, too cold, etc.

☐ Behavioural factors, e.g. where employees decide to keep output at a certain level because they are afraid that to produce more may result in the management amending their bonus scheme.

☐ Using a different grade of labour from that which was planned.

The profit variance

There are many more variances than those we have looked at here. To look at all of these other variances in depth is outside the scope of this publication. The variance analysis diagram (Figure 9.6) shows how certain of the variances, e.g. overheads, can be subdivided to provide a more detailed analysis. It also shows that the net difference between all the variances is the profit variance. The profit variance is the actual profit for the period as compared with the standard profit for the actual level of activity attained.

To conclude our study we will take a look at the reconciliation of the actual and standard profit figures.

EXAMPLE 9.2   Reconciliation of the profit variance

The data given in Table 9.4 relates to Le Wik plc for 19–3, the period which has just ended.

Comment

Observations regarding the prices from the initial data provided above reveal the details shown in Table 9.5. Note that the standard is for a different level of activity from that which was planned and this will have to be taken into account.

Answer

Firstly, we need to calculate the standard profit for the actual level of activity, as shown in Table 9.6.

Next, we add or deduct the variances to the standard profit shown in Table 9.6 to work back to the actual profit (i.e. to reconcile the two profits).

Variances (£000)

sales margin price variance
= price variance per unit (20p) × actual quantity sold (16,000 units)
= 3.2 (Favourable)

material price variance
= price variance per kilo (15p) × actual quantity used (68,000 kilos)
= 10.2 (Favourable)

material usage variance
= standard usage (64,000 kilos) *less* actual usage (68,000 kilos) × standard cost (£1.90)
= (7.6) (Adverse)

labour rate variance
= rate difference (25p per hour) × actual hours (7,200)
= (1.8) (Adverse)

labour efficiency variance
= standard hours (8,000) *less* actual hours (7,200) × standard rate (£7.50)
= 6 (Favourable)

overheads
= standard (£40,000) *less* actual (£45,000)
= (5) (Adverse)

actual profit
= standard profit (18.4) + sales margin price variance (3.2) + material price variance (10.2) − material usage variance (7.6) − labour rate variance (1.8) + labour efficiency variance (6.0) − overheads (5)
= 23.4

This can be presented in tabular form as illustrated by Table 9.7.

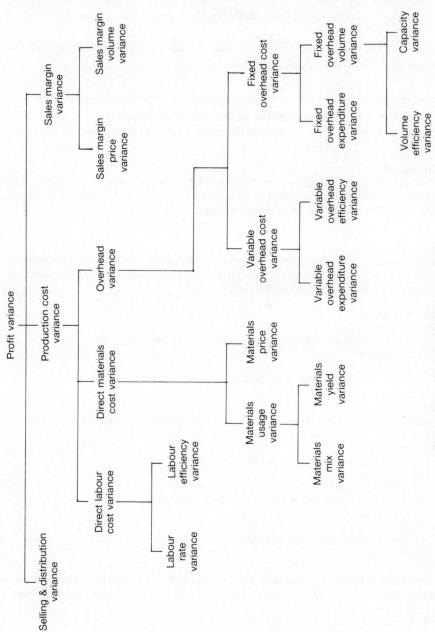

Figure 9.6   Standard costing variances

Table 9.4 Le Wik plc: budget/actual data

	Budget			Actual	
Sales (units) Budget	20,000			16,000	
	£000	£000		£000	£000
Sales (£15 per unit)		300	(£15.20 per unit)		243.2
less Costs:					
Materials (80,000 kilos)	152		(68,000 kilos)	119	
@ £1.90			@ £1.75		
Labour (10,000 hours)	75		(7,200 hours)	55.8	
@ £7.50			@ £7.75		
Overheads	40	267		45	219.8
Profit		33			23.4

Table 9.5 Le Wik plc: price variance observations

	Standard per unit (£)	Actual per unit (£)	Price variances (£)	Adverse (A) or Favourable (F)	
Sales	15	15.20	20p per unit	(F)	More revenue
Materials	1.90	1.75	15p per kilo	(F)	Lower cost
Labour	7.50	7.75	25p per hour	(A)	Higher cost

Table 9.6 Le Wik plc: calculation of the budgeted profit for the actual level of activity

		Budget	
	Units	£000	£000
Sales (original target)	20,000 @ £15		300
less Sales margin			
Volume variance	4,000 @ £15		60
Actual sales level	16,000 @ £15		240
less Standard cost of 16,000 units:			
Materials (used at 4 kilos per unit)			
= 64,000 kilos @ £1.90		121.6	
Labour (used at ½ hour per unit)			
= 8,000 hours @ £7.50		60	
Overheads (assumed no change)		40	221.6
Standard profit for 16,000 units			18.4

Now for a review and recap of our cost statement/reconciliation.

☐ The actual profit of £23,400 for 16,000 units had to be compared with the standard for 16,000 units of £18,400.

Table 9.7 Profit reconciliation statement (for 16,000 units)

	Adverse variances	Favourable variances	
	£000	£000	£000
Standard profit			18.4
Sales margin price variance		3.2	
Material variances:			
price		10.2	
usage	(7.6)		
Labour variances:			
rate	(1.8)		
efficiency		6.0	
Overhead variance	(5.0)	___	
	(14.4)	19.4	5.0
Actual profit			23.4

- □ The volume variance is the difference between the planned level of sales, 20,000 units, and the actual level of sales, 16,000 units. In our calculation it is used to ascertain the standard sales revenue applicable to the actual number of units sold.

- □ The sales margin price variance was favourable because every unit actually sold was sold at 20p more than the planned (standard) selling price.

- □ The material price variance was favourable because every kilo used cost 15p less than the planned (standard) cost.

- □ However, material usage was more than planned and therefore, adverse, i.e. used 68,000 kilos compared with a standard usage of 64,000 kilos.

- □ The adverse labour rate variance was caused by the actual wage rate paid being 25p per hour more than the planned wage rate.

- □ With the labour efficiency variance the time taken to produce the 16,000 units was less than the planned time by 800 hours. This time saving means that the variance is favourable.

- □ The amount actually spent on overheads exceeded the planned amount, i.e. there was an adverse variance.

The essence

Cost control using standard costing

Cost control is exercised in standard costing via variance analysis. Figure 9.7 should help you to see where it fits into the cost control picture. The

Figure 9.7   Cost control using standard costing

predetermination of the standards for materials, labour, overheads and sales involves the consideration of numerous factors/data.

Standard costing developed as a result of the quest for a yardstick against which to measure/compare actual performance. A standard is therefore, a predetermined target cost or target revenue.

Variance analysis

The comparison of standard with actual results should take place at frequent intervals, e.g. monthly. The variances can be:

☐ Adverse (or negative) e.g. where the actual expenditure exceeds the standard expenditure.

☐ Favourable (or positive) e.g. where the actual expenditure is less than the standard expenditure.

These will be vice versa for sales variances. The variances can be further segregated according to whether their causes are controllable or uncontrollable.

The variance analysis in the form of reports and statements supplied to management should:

☐ Highlight controllable adverse variances. This follows the principle of management by exception. Managers are free to concentrate their time and talents towards solving problems which can have a dramatic impact upon performance. This should mean that any necessary corrective action is taken at the earliest available opportunity. It also means that managers are using their valuable time more productively.

☐ Identify and communicate the causes of certain variances.

Figure 9.8   Variance analysis: the two components

The reports and statements should be circulated to all those who are responsible for the particular variance. This control by responsibility, i.e. allocating responsibility for each variance to a particular person (e.g. the labour efficiency variance for machine group Z21 to the person in charge of that machine group), ensures that the personnel involved are all striving to keep their costs under control.

Computing the variances

The cost (total) variance is the difference between the standard cost (for the actual level of activity) and the actual cost. This can be subdivided into two sub-variances, as shown in Figure 9.8 (see also Table 9.1).

The price variance is the result of paying different actual prices from the prices/rates which were planned, i.e. the standard.

The quantity variance, over which management tends to have more control, is the difference between what the company/organization planned to use, i.e. the standard usage, and the actual quantity which was used. Taken together, the price and quantity variances add back to the cost variance, which provides a quick arithmetic check on the accuracy of the figures. Finally, it must be recognized that, after all, standards are only estimates! They must therefore, be carefully monitored – hence the need for constant feedback (see Figure 9.7) – and revised accordingly.

Further reading

Dyson, J.R., *Accounting for Non-accounting Students*, Pitman, 1994
Harper, W.M., *Cost and Management Accounting*, Pitman, 1995

10

Capital investment appraisal

Objectives

On completion of your study of this chapter, you should be able to:

□ Understand how the payback and average rate of return methods of capital investment appraisal work.

□ Know the difference between compound interest tables, the sum of an annuity of £1 tables, the present value of £1 tables and the present value of an annuity of £1 tables.

□ Use the present value of an annuity of £1 and present value of £1 tables to solve some introductory problems.

□ Understand the treatment of depreciation in the calculation of the cash flows.

□ Carry out an elementary sensitivity analysis.

□ Appreciate that there are limitations to all of the methods demonstrated.

The principal aim of this chapter is to show you how to use the present value tables to produce information which will help management with its capital investment decision making. This particular topic area is covered in much greater depth in *The Essence of Financial Management* (in this series) and numerous other financial management texts. However, please note that some authors refer to capital investment appraisal as **capital budgeting**.

Payback method

This simple approach looks at how long it takes an investment to repay its initial cost (see Table 10.1, for example).

Table 10.1 The payback method

Cost	Project P £20,000		Project Q £20,000	
Year	Cash flow* £000	Cumulative cash flow £000	Cash flow* £000	Cumulative cash flow £000
1	4	4	6	6
2	6	10	8	14
3	7	17	6	**20**
4	3	**20**	3	23
5	5	25	2	25

*The cash flows generated by the project should be the relevant cash flows. This will be explained in due course.

It can be observed that project P has a payback of four years and project Q has a payback of three years. Management tends to favour those projects which payback more quickly because the longer a project takes to repay the greater the uncertainty. The only certainty about the future is that it will be uncertain! However, this method does not take account of the time value of money, i.e. that over a period of time the value of money tends to go down, e.g. £1 now will be worth less in say three years' time.

Average rate of return method

Also called the **unadjusted rate of return** method, this is a somewhat oversimplified method which expresses the average annual net cash flow as a percentage of the original investment (see Table 10.2, for example). This return on investment type method assumes that the net cash flows generated are the same from year to year. The cash flows from both projects could fluctuate significantly from year to year and also vary significantly between each other, i.e. it does not take into account the timing of the cash flows generated. Here also, the time value of money (the fact that £1 tomorrow will be worth less than £1 today) is ignored.

Accounting rate of return

An accounting return on investment approach could also be used which expresses the financial accounting profit as a percentage of the initial or

Table 10.2 The average rate of return method

	Machine R	Machine S
Cost of machine	£100,000	£100,000
Total estimated net cash flow for 7 years (i.e. the life of the project)	£171,500	£190,400
Average annual net cash flow	£24.500	£27,200
Average rate of return	24.5%	27.2%

average amount of capital invested. This method excludes the time value of money, and ignores relevant costs/revenue.

How to use annuity tables

When confronted with a number of annuity tables for the first time, managers and executives on short courses and students soon begin to ask questions:

☐ What are all these for?
☐ How do we use them?
☐ Why use this table and not that one?
☐ Which of these should we use to discount the cash flows?
☐ What do they tell us?
☐ Which of these do we use for capital investment appraisal?

Well, let us have a look at some of them and attempt to answer this kind of question.

The compound interest table (compound sum of £1)

Table 10.3 shows how much an investment of £1 will amount to at a certain fixed rate of interest in a certain number of years' time (see Table 10.3).

Table 10.3 tells us how much £1 invested now at, say, 12% will amount to in, say, five years' time, i.e. rate column 12%, year 5 = £1.76p to the nearest 1p, as indicated by the 1.762 which was highlighted. Each year the interest is re-invested and also generates interest as illustrated in Table 10.4.

If you invest a sum of money at a fixed rate of interest for a specific period of time all you have to do is multiply the sum invested with the appropriate rate given by the table.

Table 10.3　Compound sum of £1 (extract from tables)

Year	10%	12%	14%	16%	18%	20%
1	1.100	1.120	1.140	1.160	1.180	1.200
2	1.210	1.254	1.300	1.346	1.392	1.440
3	1.331	1.405	1.482	1.561	1.643	1.728
4	1.464	1.574	1.689	1.811	1.939	2.074
5	1.611	**1.762**	1.925	2.100	2.288	2.488
6	**1.772**	1.974	2.195	2.436	2.700	2.986

Table 10.4　Compound interest on £1

		Investment £
Example	Invest £1 today	1.00
End of year 1	Interest @ 10% × £1	0.10
Cumulative		1.10
End of year 2	Interest @ 10% × £1.10	0.11
Cumulative		1.21
End of year 3	Interest @ 10% × £1.21	0.12
Cumulative		1.33p　and so on

EXAMPLE 10.1　Compound interest

To invest £1,500 today at 10% for six years would accumulate to £2,658 at the end of the sixth year. This is computed as follows:

Rate 10% for 6 years		Amount invested now	
1.772	×	£1,500	= £2,658

In addition to working out the amount accumulated, this table can be used to produce an **opportunity cost**, i.e. the value of the benefit forgone. For example, an amount invested in a business project could have alternatively been invested in a bank, or government stock, or financial institution.

Investing an annual sum (sum of an annuity of £1 for N years)

From a review of Table 10.5 it can be observed that it shows what happens if £1 is invested at the end of each year, at a fixed rate of interest, and for a certain number of years.

Table 10.5   The sum of an annuity of £1 for N years (extract from tables)

Year	10%	12%	14%	16%	18%	20%
1	1.000	1.000	1.000	1.000	1.000	1.000
2	2.100	2.120	2.140	2.160	2.180	2.200
3	3.310	3.374	3.440	3.506	3.572	3.640
4	4.641	4.779	4.921	5.066	5.215	5.368
5	6.105	6.353	6.610	**6.877**	7.154	7.442
6	7.716	8.115	**8.536**	8.977	9.442	9.930

EXAMPLE 10.2   Investment

An investment of £1, at the end of *each* year for six years (i.e. an annual investment of £1) at 14% would produce £8.54p to the nearest 1p. This builds up as shown in Table 10.6.

Table 10.6   Compound interest for an annual investment of £1

		Investment
End of year 1	Annual investment	1.00
End of year 2	Interest @ 14% × £1	0.14
	Annual investment	1.00
		2.14
End of year 3	Interest @ 14% × £2.14	0.30
	Annual investment	1.00
		3.44 and so on

Notice that the table is drawn up on the assumption that *the investment is made at the end of each year*.

If a fixed amount of money is to be invested at the end of each year the annual amount is multiplied by the appropriate rate which is given in Table 10.5, according to the rate at which the amount is invested and the length of time involved.

EXAMPLE 10.3   Investment of £2,000

To invest an annual amount of £2,000 at the end of each year for five years at 16% would compound (i.e. accumulate) to £13,754. This is computed as follows:

Rate 16% for 5 years   annual investment
      6.877   ×   £2,000   = £13,754

Thus, although the amount invested is only £10,000 (i.e £2,000 per year × 5 years), it generates an additional £3,754 because of the accumulation of the compound interest.

Table 10.7 Present value of £1 (extract from tables)

Year	10%	12%	14%	16%	18%	20%
1	**0.909**	0.893	0.877	0.862	0.847	0.833
2	0.826	0.797	0.769	0.743	0.718	0.694
3	**0.751**	0.712	0.675	0.641	0.609	0.579
4	0.683	0.636	0.592	0.552	0.516	0.482
5	0.621	0.567	0.519	0.476	**0.437**	0.402
6	0.564	**0.507**	0.456	0.410	0.370	0.335

The present value table (present value of £1)

From a capital investment appraisal point of view, this is the most important and most frequently used table (see Table 10.7).

This table is all about the **time value of money**, i.e. the fact that over a period of time the value of money will tend to decrease.

The table can be looked at in two ways:

1. It shows us *how much we need to invest at a specific fixed rate of interest and for a particular period of time to produce £1*, e.g. if we want to produce £1 at the end of year 1 at a 10% rate of interest we have to invest 90.9p at the beginning of year 1, as follows:

Investment (to nearest 1p) at the start of the year   = 91p
At the end of year (to nearest 1p) interest @ 10% × 91p   = 9p

∴ investment + interest   = £1

or if we want to produce £1 in six years at a 12% rate of interest we would have to invest 0.507p now (51p to the nearest 1p). This, together with the compound interest would produce £1 at the end of year 6 (as indicated by the 0.507 figure which is highlighted in Table 10.7).

2. The other way of looking at the table is that it tells us *what the value of £1 receivable in a certain number of years' time, taking into account a specific rate of interest, will be*, i.e. the present value of receiving £1 in the future.

In capital investment appraisal, this philosophy is the one which is followed, as it tends to explain the time value of money. For example the present value of £1 receivable in five years' time and taking into account a rate of interest of 18% is .437p (or 44p to the nearest 1p) or the present value £1 receivable in three years' time at a rate of interest of 10% is .751p (or 75p to the nearest 1p), (see Table 10.7).

The value of £1 received today is £1 but if you receive it in the future its value will tend to be less than a pound. The rate of interest could be in line

Table 10.8 Present value of an annuity of £1 (extract)

Year	10%	12%	14%	16%	18%	20%
1	0.909	0.893	0.877	0.862	0.847	0.833
2	1.736	1.690	1.647	1.605	1.566	1.528
3	2.487	2.402	2.322	2.246	2.174	2.106
4	3.170	3.037	2.914	**2.798**	2.690	2.589
5	3.791	3.605	3.433	3.274	3.127	2.991
6	4.355	4.111	3.889	3.685	3.498	3.326

with the rate of inflation or the company/organization's cost of capital or the required rate of return for the type of project which is being reviewed.

The present value of an annuity table

This table can also be used in capital investment appraisal for certain situations (see Table 10.8).

It can also be viewed in two ways:

1. It tells us how much we need to invest now, at a specific fixed rate of interest, to generate £1 at the end of *each* year for a specified number of years. For example if we wish to receive £1 at the end of each of the next four years, and taking interest into account at 16%, we would have to invest £2.798 (£2.80p), i.e. £2.80 invested now at 16% will generate £1 per year at the end of each of the next four years.

2. It represents *the present value of receiving the same amount each year for a certain number of years*, and taking interest into account at a specific rate. It can be used to find out the time value of cash flows, but only in cases where the same amount is received each year for a number of years, and is therefore of limited application.

Present value tables

In capital investment appraisal, the time value of money is taken into account by revaluing the cash flows at their present values. The appraisal process will involve the following:

□ The estimation of the cash flows over the life of the project. The cash flows to be estimated, should be the **relevant/incremental cash flows**, i.e. they take account only of those items of income or expenditure which come in or go out if the project goes ahead; e.g. if a new employee has to

Table 10.9 Capital investment appraisal: risk categories

Risk category	Required rate of return
Low	12%
Medium	16%
High	20%

be taken on if a particular project goes ahead, the remuneration paid to the new employee is a relevant/incremental cost.

☐ Taking into account taxation.

☐ Selecting the rate of interest which is to be used as the discount rate. A company/organization could opt for:

(a) the cost of capital; or

(b) a rate which takes into account the risk category of the project (see Table 10.9, for example); or

(c) a cut-off rate. If the net present value of a project's cash flows, as discounted using the cut-off rate, is negative the project will not go ahead.

We will now proceed to work through a series of problems and self-check assignments to illustrate how the present value tables are used.

More detailed present value tables can be found on pages 161–169. However, for the examples which follow we will use the table extracts which have been included so far.

EXAMPLE 10.4 Using the tables

Machinery can be purchased on payment of the following amounts:

☐ £5,000 immediately, and

☐ £2,000 at the end of each of the next four years, and

☐ £4,000 at the end of the fifth year.

Using the appropriate tables, calculate the present value/equivalent cash price which could be offered, if payment were to be made in full now. Compound interest needs to be taken into account at 10% per annum.

Answer

It will cost £6,340 at 10% per annum compound interest now to produce the four annual instalments of £2,000 each. £2,484 will need to be invested now at 10% per annum compound interest to generate the £4,000 which will be required at the end of year 5.

Table 10.10 Calculating the equivalent cash price using present value tables

	£
Amount payable immediately	5,000
Present value of an annuity of £2,000 for 4 years @ 10%	
= £2,000 × 3.170 (Table 10.8)	6,340
Present value of £4,000 at the end of 5 years @ 10%	
= £4,000 × 0.621 (Table 10.7)	2,484
Present value (equivalent cash price)	13,824
This is the cost of producing	5,000 now
plus £2,000 × 4 =	8,000
and £4,000 × 1 =	4,000
	17,000

 SELF-ASSESSMENT QUESTION 10.1

Now see if you can solve a similar problem which is described in the following.

The equivalent cash price
Your company is considering buying some equipment and has received an offer from one of the suppliers involving the payment of:

□ £3,000 on delivery, and

□ £3,000 at the end of each of the next three years, and

□ £5,000 at the end of year 4, and

□ £2,500 at the end of year 5.

The interest rate applicable is 12%.
   When you have finished your calculations please turn to pages 158–159 and compare your answer with the suggested answer.

Depreciation and cash flows

When we studied cash budgeting it was noted that *depreciation is a non-cash item*. The cash moves when you either buy or sell an asset, *not* when you charge depreciation in the accounts. Therefore, the estimated cash flows from projects should not include a deduction for depreciation. However, if the cash flows have had depreciation deducted the depreciation will have to be added back. Also note that from a cash flow point of view it is *not* the profit or loss on the sale of the asset that should be included in the cash flow but the actual sale proceeds. The actual cash received is the cash inflow.

Depreciation is a non-cash item.

EXAMPLE 10.5   Cash flows of the same amount per year and depreciation

The forecast incremental receipts and payments applicable to the purchase of a new machine are as shown in Table 10.11.

Table 10.11   Identical cash flows

Year	1 £000	2 £000	3 £000	4 £000
Receipts	16	16	16	16
less Payments*	14	14	14	14
Net income	2	2	2	2

*The payments include depreciation at £5,000 per year. The company's cost of capital is 10%.

The new machine will cost £20,000.

Answer

First of all we adjust the net income figures for each year, by adding back the depreciation (see Table 10.12).

Table 10.12   Adjusting for depreciation

Year	1 £000	2 £000	3 £000	4 £000
Net income	2	2	2	2
add back Depreciation	5	5	5	5
Net cash flow	7	7	7	7

Because the cash flows are the same each year, we can use Table 10.8, the present value of an annuity of £1, to discount the cash flows, as follows:

annual net cash flows × discount rate = present value
(£7,000)   (3.17)   (£22,190)

```
┌─────────────────┐
│ The present value│
│ of the cash flows│
└─────────────────┘
```

Less

```
┌─────────────────┐
│  The initial cost│
│  of the project  │
└─────────────────┘
```

=

```
┌─────────────────┐
│ The net present  │
│  value (NPV)     │
└─────────────────┘
```

Figure 10.1 The net present value of a project

We can deduct the initial cost of the project:

less initial investment (£20,000) = **Net present value (NPV)** = **£2,190**

The NPV is positive and the project is therefore worthy of acceptance/further consideration.

From the above, it can be observed that the net present value (NPV) of a project is as shown in Figure 10.1.

 SELF-ASSESSMENT QUESTION 10.2

Identical cash flows/the treatment of depreciation

If the GT Company go ahead with a new project they anticipate that their net cash flows (before deducting depreciation) over a six-year period will be £12,000 per annum. The project would involve buying specialized equipment costing £60,000 which would be depreciated at £10,000 per annum and have no residual value at the end of year six. Their cost of capital is 16%.

See if you can calculate the net present value of this project and indicate if it is worthy of further consideration.

When you have completed your attempt at this problem, turn to page 159 and compare it with the suggested solution.

In the real world of business, however, it is more likely that the estimated cash flows which result from taking on a new project will vary from year to year. This means, that each individual amount will have to be discounted using the appropriate present value of £1 as illustrated in Table 10.7.

EXAMPLE 10.6   Fluctuating cash flows

Wys plc are considering purchasing a new robotic machine. The anticipated receipts and payments resulting from its purchase are as shown in Table 10.13.

Table 10.13   Fluctuating cash flows

Year	1 £000	2 £000	3 £000	4 £000	5 £000
Incremental receipts	14	16	22	12	9
Incremental payments*	11	15	16	10	8

*Includes depreciation of £4,000 per annum.

An immediate cash outlay of £20,000 is needed to finance the purchase. The company's cost of capital is 16%.

Answer

The NPV is positive, which means that the project is worthy of consideration. Note, that the cash flows had to be adjusted because depreciation had been included in the payment figures.

Table 10.14   The net present value of fluctuating cash flows

Year	Receipts £000	Payments* £0000	Cash flow £000	Discount factor £000	Net present value £000
1	14	7	7	0.862	6.034
2	16	11	5	0.743	3.715
3	22	12	10	0.641	6.410
4	12	6	6	0.552	3.312
5	9	4	5	0.476	2.380
					21.851
		less initial outlay		20,000	
		Net present value		**1.851**	

*Adjusted for depreciation.

Discounting the cash flows in this way may also be described as discounted cash flow (DCF).

Why in the above answer did we say worthy of consideration rather than acceptance? The reason for this caution is that the financial data are just one part of the capital investment, decision-making jigsaw. There are many non-financial factors which have to be taken into account, e.g. reliability, the efficiency of the supplier's after sales service, standardization, etc.

Now see if you can complete the final activity problem.

SELF-ASSESSMENT QUESTION 10.3

Becwik Ltd

The directors of Becwik Ltd are considering the acquisition of a new machine which could generate incremental cash inflows and outflows as shown in Table 10.15. The immediate initial outlay to acquire the machine and set it up for operations is estimated at £79,000 and it will have no residual value at the end of year six. (For financial accounting purposes new machinery is depreciated on a straight-line basis). Becwik's corporate planning team has categorized all projects as shown in Table 10.16. The risk category of this project is considered to be average.

Table 10.15 Becwik Ltd: incremental cash flows

Year	1 £000	2 £000	3 £000	4 £000	5 £000
Income	40	60	80	80	30
Expenditure before depreciation	30	40	40	30	20
Incremental cash flow	10	20	40	50	10

Table 10.16 Becwik Ltd: risk categories

Risk	Required rate of return
A Low	10%
B Average	14%
C High	18%

You are required to evaluate the project.

When you have attempted to answer the above problem, please turn to page 160 and compare it with the suggested answer.

Residual values

If the machinery or equipment under review has a residual value at the end of the project this should be included as an additional cash flow for the period in which it is to be received. However, beware! Many examples in numerous texts assume that the residual value will be received at the end of the year in which the project comes to an end. In reality, when the project does come to an end, it may be some time before the machinery or equipment is disposed of. The cash from such a disposal should therefore be included as a cash flow of the year in which it is anticipated that it will be received.

Taxation

In producing the cash flows the tax factor should be taken into account *assuming that the company will be paying tax* as follows:

☐ The tax benefit (i.e. the tax allowance at the tax paying businesses rate of tax) should be deducted from the cash flows of the period in which the benefit is received as a repayment or used to reduce the amount of tax which has to be paid over.

☐ The tax payable on income, e.g. taxable cash flows received and taxable profits on the disposal of machinery and equipment, should be deducted from the cash flows received (if any) of the period in which the tax will be actually paid over.

In both of the above cases there is usually a time lag between the period to which the benefit/tax payable relates, and the period which derives the benefit or in which the tax is paid.

Other methods

☐ *Discounted payback*
The payback method referred to earlier in this chapter can also be computed using the present value of the cash flows. The discounted payback period is the time that it takes for the cumulative present value of the cash flows to equal the initial investment.

☐ *Internal rate of return (IRR)*
This is also called the **yield method**: the internal rate of return is the discount rate which will discount the cash flows to a net present value of nil (i.e. the present value of the cash flows less the initial investment = a nil NPV). It is, therefore, a return on investment approach, the IRR being an indication of what a particular project is likely to earn.

Sensitivity analysis

This is a method of assessing the extent to which a change in one or more of the assumptions on which a capital investment project (or a budget) was based, would affect the outcome. For example, higher or lower than expected wage settlements, machine running costs, and residual values of plant disposed of could significantly affect the possible outcome.

This enables management to review a number of possible outcomes particularly in situations where the exact outcome is difficult to predict, and thereby assist them with their decision making.

Which method?

The methods which use the net present value tables are to be preferred because they all take into account the time value of money. However, it must be stressed that the selection of a discount rate is not always an easy task, e.g. there are a number of ways of calculating a company's cost of capital. With all methods, it must be remembered that the cash flows/residual values of machinery and equipment are only estimates.

The essence

Relevant/incremental cash flows

The methods described in this chapter all depend upon the predetermination of the cash flows. Thus you should always be aware that the cash flows used in capital investment appraisal (also called **capital budgeting**) are only estimates. Their accuracy will depend upon the data and the validity of the assumptions used in their preparation. The cash flows which are to be used should be relevant/incremental cash flows (see also Chapter 1).

Examples of relevant/incremental cash flows are as follows. If as a result of taking on a new project:

- A new worker has to be employed and paid £15,000 per year.
- A special maintenance contract has to be purchased at a cost of £2,400 per year.
- Certain materials have to be purchased.
- Residual value/scrap value is received at the end of the project's life.

Examples of irrelevant costs are:

- If a supervisor is paid a salary of £18,000 per annum whether or not the project is undertaken.
- Factory rent and rates which have to be paid whether or not the project under review goes ahead.

Note that when estimating the cash flows, *depreciation* which is a non-cash item should be ignored.

The time value of money

This means that £1 tomorrow will be worth less than £1 today. Thus, cash flows which are to be received in the future are not worth as much as they are now.

The financial information provided – a warning

From the outset it should be noted that the financial information provided to management forms just one of the many component parts needed to effectively vet a capital investment proposal. Indeed, there are numerous non-financial factors which have to be taken into account, e.g. efficiency of servicing, reliability, risks associated with buying from overseas suppliers, etc.

The tables

If you are to master capital investment appraisal you need to be able to use the following:

☐ The present value of £1 table, an extract of which is shown as Table 10.7 in this chapter.
☐ The present value of an annuity of £1 table, an extract of which appears as Table 10.8 in this chapter.

Methods of capital investment appraisal

We can classify the methods of capital investment appraisal/capital budgeting in a number of ways. For this introductory study, I suggest that we simply divide the methods into those which do *not* take into account the time value of money, and those which *do* take into account the time value of money.

Methods which do not take the time value of money into account
☐ *Payback*
    This method calculates how long it takes the cash flows generated by a specific project to recover the initial cost of the investment. Those who

use this method of evaluation prefer those projects which repay the cost of the initial investment in the shortest time. In estimating the cash flows the earlier cash flows are likely to be more accurate than later cash flows.

□ *The average rate of return (unadjusted rate of return)*
This return on investment method expresses the average cash flow per year as a percentage of the initial investment. Although it is simple to calculate it must be pointed out that it does ignore the timing of the cash flows, i.e. it averages the cash flows over the life of the project when in fact they could fluctuate quite significantly from year to year.

□ *Accounting rate of return*
This method uses financial accounting profits.

Each of the above methods suffer because they ignore the time value of money. The timing of the cash flows, i.e. the year in which the money comes in, or goes out can have a dramatic impact upon a project.

Methods which take account of the time value of money

□ *The net present value method*
To find the net present value (NPV) each of the cash flows is multiplied by the appropriate discount factor, using Table 10.7 (the present value of £1 table). These are then added up and the initial investment deducted. If the resulting figure, the NPV, is positive the project is worthy of consideration; if the NPV is negative the project should be rejected because it is not a wealth-creating opportunity. Note that when using this method, if all the cash flows are identical, Table 10.8, the present value of an annuity of £1 table, could be used and would save calculation time. This discounting process may also be called DCF (discounted cash flow).

□ *The internal rate of return (IRR) or yield method*
Although to produce numerate examples of this is outside the scope of this introduction, it is worth noting that this method is important. Look at any financial management text and you will find out why. The internal rate of return is the discount rate which will produce an NPV of nil, i.e. the cash flows discounted less the initial cost of the machine/equipment/ project = nil (it equates the cost and revenue). Therefore projects with an IRR greater than the company's normal discount rate appropriate to the particular project under review are well worth further investigation.

□ *Discounted payback*
This method simply calculates the payback using the discounted cash flows.

The above methods which take into account the time value of money are preferable to those which do not.

Taxation

Taxation allowances must be included in the cash flows for the period which benefits from those allowances. Tax payments must be included in the cash flows for the period in which they are to be paid over. Thus care needs to be exercised in taking the tax factor into account by taking the various time lags into account, e.g. the tax on the income of year 1 could be paid in year 2.

Sensitivity analysis

Sensitivity analysis can provide management with a range of possible outcomes resulting from one or more changes in the basic assumptions on which the data used is based.

Further reading

Atrill, P. and E. McLaney, *Financial Management Accounting for Non-specialists*, Prentice Hall, 1997

Chadwick, L. and D. Kirkby, *Financial Management*, Routledge, 1996

Myddleton, D.C., *The Essence of Financial Management*, Prentice Hall, 1995

Pike, R., and B. Neale, *Corporate Finance and Investment*, Prentice Hall, 1996

Appendix 1

Suggested answers to self assessment questions

Chapter 4: Throngfirth Manufacturing

See Table A.1 (overleaf) for answer to Question 1.
See Table A.2 for answers to Questions 2 and 3.

Points to note (not part of the answer)

Relating to Table A.1 and A.2.

- Firstly, notice that I have lumped together those overheads which are shared out according to the same method of apportionment, e.g. buildings insurance and lighting are both shared up according to floor area.
- The total column provides a cross-add which acts as a check on the arithmetic accuracy of the figures.
- I have used the word allocate to mean an overhead which can be directly associated with a department/cost centre, and apportionment to denote those overheads which cannot be identified with a specific department/ cost centre. You should note that other authors do not attempt to draw such a fine distinction between these words.
- Also, even though we know the direct labour hours for the machine department, we do not use them to work out the overhead absorption rate. Why? Because the machine department overheads are being recovered using a rate per machine hour.
- Again, note that we use the 15 machine hours to compute the machine department overheads applicable to product PQ.

Table A.1 Throngfirth Manufacturing: departmental overhead summary/analysis

Overheads	Total £	Production departments			Service departments	
		Machine £	Paint £	Assembly £	Stores £	Power £
Indirect materials & labour (allocated)	91,700	36,730	11,270	11,900	16,680	15,120
Fuel (allocated)	74,000	–	–	–	–	74,000
Buildings insurance & lighting (floor area)	9,600	4,800 $(8/16)$	1,200 $(2/16)$	2,400 $(4/16)$	600 $(1/16)$	600 $(1/16)$
Supervision & Canteen (No. of employees)	43,200	12,960 $(6/20)$	4,320 $(2/20)$	17,280 $(8/20)$	4,320 $(2/20)$	4,320 $(2/20)$
Machinery insurance (value of machines)	4,800	2,880 $(3/5)$	960 $(1/5)$	–	–	960 $(1/5)$
Depreciation (allocated)	25,700	12,400	6,300	2,100	1,400	3,500
	249,000	69,770	24,050	33,680	23,000	98,500
Stores (technical estimates)		5,750	5,750	9,200	–23,000	2,300
Power (technical estimates)		60,480	25,200	15,120		–100,800
	£249,000	£136,000	£55,000	£58,000		
Overhead absorption rates						
Machine hours		$\dfrac{20,000}{=£6.80}$				
Direct labour hours			$\dfrac{5,000}{=£11.00}$	$\dfrac{8,000}{=£7.25}$		

Table A.2   Throngfirth Manufacturing: calculation of the proposed selling price of product PQ

		£	£
Direct materials			1,277
Direct labour			
(4 hrs × £9)	Machine dept	36	
(3 hrs × £8)	Paint dept	24	
(16 hrs × £7)	Assembly dept	112	172
Overheads			
(15 hrs × £6.80)	Machine dept	102	
(3 hrs × £11)	Paint dept	33	
(16 hrs × £7.25)	Assembly dept	116	251
	Product cost		1,700
add Mark up (40% × £1,700) =			680
	Proposed selling price		2,380

☐ Finally, when you select a basis of apportionment, e.g. floor area, etc., you have to select the basis which is most appropriate for sharing out the particular item of overhead expenditure concerned.

Chapter 5: Heaton Postex plc

See Table A.3 for the answer to Question 1.

Table A.3   Heaton Postex plc: marginal costing statement

	Current position 19–3		Next year 19–4	
	Per unit £	40,000 units £000	Per unit £	50,000 units £000
Selling price	120	4,800	125	6,250
less variable cost	96	3,840	100	5,000
Contribution	24	960	25(20%)	1,250
(Proof £24 × 40,000)			(proof £25×50,000)	
less Fixed costs		164		186
Profit		796		1,064

See Table A.4 for Question 2.

The contribution needed to produce a profit of £796 in Table A.3 would be as shown in Table A.5 (Question 3).

The answer to Question 4 is in Table A.6.

Table A.4   Heaton Postex plc: breakeven points

	19–3 £000	19–4 £000
Fixed costs	164	186
Profit volume ratio (as above)	20%	20%
Breakeven point	£000	£000
(Fixed cost ÷ PV ratio) =	820 =	930

Table A.5   Heaton Postex plc: sales needed to achieve profit target

	£000
Fixed costs 19–4	186
add Profit	796
Contribution required	982

The number of units which must be sold to produce the contribution required is therefore

$$\frac{\text{contribution required}}{\text{contribution per unit}} = \frac{£982,000}{£25} = 39,280 \text{ units}$$

£000
This has a sales value of 39,280 units × £125 = 4,910 (Question 3)

Table A.6   Heaton Postex plc: amount available for additional fixed costs

		£000
The total contribution from the sale of 56,000 units @ £25 per unit would be		1,400
	£000	
less Fixed costs	186	
Profit target	1,200	1,386
Amount available for additional fixed costs		14

Points to note (not part of the answer)

Relating to Tables A.3 to A.6 inclusive.

□ Good layout and presentation should make the information produced more understandable.

- The contributions in (1) of £960,000 and £1,250,000 and (4) of £1,400,000 could be calculated quickly by multiplying the units sold by the contribution per unit.

- The profit volume ratio, i.e. the contribution as a percentage of sales, can be used to calculate the breakeven point. However, other methods are quite acceptable.

- Both parts (3) and (4) involve the use of the technique designed to help with profit target problems, i.e. the knowledge that the contribution required equals the fixed costs plus the profit target.

- In (4) a comparison is made between the contribution which is expected and the contribution which is needed, the difference being the amount which is available to spend on additional fixed costs.

Chapter 5: Scoubado Manufacturing

See Tables A.7 and A.8.

Table A.7 Scoubado Manufacturing: marginal costing/key factor analysis (first output level)

	J	K	L
Output level (first)	up to 30 units	up to 24 units	up to 60 units
	£	£	£
Selling price	75	108	59
less Variable cost	50	84	39
Contribution	25	24	20
Production per hour (units)	x	x	x
	2	1.33	3
	=	=	=
Contribution per hour	£50	£32	£60

The ranking in terms of the highest contribution per hour is:

1. L up to 60 units £60.
2. J up to 30 units £50.
3. J over 30 units £44.
4. K up to 24 units £32.
5. L over 60 units £30.
6. K over 24 units £28.

Table A.8 Scoubado Manufacturing: marginal costing/key factor analysis (second output level)

		J over 30 units £	K over 24 units £	L over 60 units £
	Selling price	72	105	49
less	Variable cost	50	84	39
	Contribution	£22	£21	£10
Production per hour (units)		x	x	x
		2	1.33	3
		=	=	=
	Contribution per hour	£44	£28	£30

The maximum contribution per day is as shown in Table A.9.

Table A.9 Scoubado Manufacturing: maximum contribution per day

Product	Quantity	Time per unit	Total time (hours)	Contribution per hour	Total
	units	mins		£	£
L	60	20	20	60	1,200
J	30	30	15	50	750
			35		
J	14	30	7	44	308
			42 hours		2,258

Points to note (not part of the answer)

□ The reductions in the selling prices for J, K and L respectively are matched by a reduction in their contribution per unit of the same amount.

□ The key factor (limiting factor) in this problem was the productive time available.

□ The above solution therefore answered the question, 'Which combination of products will maximize the contribution per day if there are only 42 hours of production time available?'

□ When the total hours needed reached 35 hours, the final question which had to be answered was, 'With the seven hours left and using the third ranked contribution, how many units can be produced?' (Seven hours at half an hour per unit = 14 units.)

Chapter 5: Holme Honley Products plc

The breakeven chart (Question 1) is shown in Figure A.1, which also indicates the margin of safety. Table A.10 answers Question 2.

Figure A.1 Holme Honley Products plc: breakeven chart

Table A.10 Holme Honley Products plc: calculation of the breakeven point

	Per unit £		25,000 units £000		15,000 units £000
Selling price	100		2,500		1,500
less Variable cost	40		1,000		600
Contribution	60	(60% PV ratio)	1,500		900
less Fixed costs			1,200		1,200
Profit			300	(Loss)	(300)

Breakeven point (£000)
= fixed cost ÷ PV ratio

$= £1,200 \times \dfrac{100}{60} = £2,000$

Breakeven point (in 000 units)

$= \dfrac{\text{fixed cost}}{\text{contribution}} = \dfrac{£1,200}{£60} = 20$

Points to note (not part of the answer)

☐ The horizontal scale of the breakeven chart can be expressed in terms of output or level of activity.

☐ The breakeven point can be worked out mathematically, in terms of value and output/level of activity.

☐ To read off the position for a particular level of activity from the breakeven chart, all you have to do is project a vertical line upwards (e.g. at 60%) to see where it crosses the fixed cost line, the total cost line and the sales line. The gap between the £1,800 total cost and the sales revenue of £1,500 represents the loss of £300.

Chapter 6: Oldwik & Co. Ltd

In the Oldwik & Co. Ltd example, the under- and over-absorption of overheads (Question 1) is the result of the actual number of units being produced being different from the budgeted number of units produced. The overhead absorption rate was calculated:

$$\frac{\text{budgeted fixed overhead}}{\text{budgeted production (units)}} = \frac{£27,500}{25,000} = £1.10\text{p per unit}$$

Thus, every time one unit is produced £1.10p will be added to costs in order to recover the fixed overheads.

In the example it was assumed that the actual fixed overheads would be the same as the budget, i.e. £27,500. Therefore, if the actual volume produced is less than the budget, the fixed overheads included in the product costs will be less than the £27,500, i.e. there will be an *under-recovery of fixed overheads*. Conversely, if the actual number of units produced exceeds the budget, then the fixed overheads included in the product costs will be greater than £27,500, i.e. there will be an *over-recovery*. They can be computed as shown in Table A.11.

Comment

You should note that there could also be a difference between the budgeted and actual fixed overheads. However, the above answer does apply to other methods of overhead absorption, e.g. machine hour rates and direct labour hour rates etc.

Table A.11 Absorption v. marginal: over- and under-absorption

	Production units		Period 1
Budget	25,000		
Actual	26,000		
Over budget	1,000	× £1.10p =	£1,100 over-absorbed
	Production units		Period 2
Budget	25,000		
Actual	23,000		
Under budget	2,000	× £1.10p =	£2,200 under-absorbed

The accounting treatment of under- and over-absorption of overheads (Question 2) is quite straightforward.

☐ An **under-absorption** represents an under charge for the overheads, it must therefore be *deducted* in computing the profit.

☐ An **over-absorption** means that the charge for overheads was too high, so to put matters right it must be *added back* on to the profits.

In Period 1 the effect of including the fixed overheads (5,000 units × £1.10) of £5,500 in the closing stock (Question 3) was to increase the absorption costing profit by that amount to £16,700, as compared with the marginal costing profit of £11,200. The £5,500 being treated as a deferred expense in absorption costing but written off as a 'period cost' in marginal costing.

Thus, in absorption costing, the fixed overheads included in the closing stock for an accounting period will increase the profits for that period when compared with marginal costing. However, any fixed overheads included in the opening stock for a period will reduce the absorption costing profit for that period when compared with marginal costing, e.g. the £5,500 in Period 2.

The net difference between the absorption costing and marginal costing profit will, therefore, depend upon the overheads included in both the opening stock and closing stock (see Table A.12). For an example from Period 2.

Table A.12 Absorption v. marginal: profit difference reconciliation using fixed overheads carried and brought forward

Period 2	£
Fixed overheads carried forward via the closing stock	1,100
less Fixed overheads brought forward via the opening stock	5,500
(Absorption profit £23,000 − marginal profit £27,400)	(4,400)

Operating statement (absorption costing) for quarter to 31 March 19–4				£	£
Sales (19,500 units @ £24)					468,000
less					
Cost of sales:					
	Units		Total cost		
Opening stock	3,000	@	£20	60,000	
add Production	21,000	@	£20	420,000	
	24,000	@	£20	480,000	
less Closing stock	4,500	@	£20	90,000	390,000*
Gross profit	19,500	@	£4		78,000
add back Over-absorption**					5,000
					83,000
less Selling & distribution expenses					29,000
			Profit		54,000

*This cost of sales figure is equal to 19,500 units at £20 per unit
**The company produced 1,000 units in excess of its budget. It therefore included 1,000 units × £5 fixed cost per unit too much i its cost figures: i.e. fixed overheads absorbed 21,000 × £5 = £105,000, less actual fixed overheads of £100,000 = £5,000 over absorbed

Figure A.2   Operating statement (absorption costing)

Chapter 6: Kim plc

See Figures A.2 and A.3 for the answer to Question 1.

The difference between the two profit figures (Question 2) is caused by the inclusion of fixed costs in both the opening and closing stock valuations and can be reconciled as shown in Table A.13. Alternatively, this can also be explained by looking at the differences between the stock figures, as shown in Table A.14.

Comments (not part of the answer)

In absorption costing the total cost of £20 per unit (inclusive of fixed costs @ £5 per unit) was used to make the operating statement calculations easier and clearer. The gross profit of (selling price £24 less total cost £20) £4 per unit × 19,500 units sold = £78,000 gross profit and provides a quick check on the arithmetic accuracy of the figures. The contribution per unit (selling price £24 less marginal cost £15) of £9 per unit × 19,500 units sold = £175,500 and provides a check on the arithmetic accuracy of the contribution figure.

Operating statement (marginal costing) for quarter to 31 March 19–4					£	£
Sales (19,500 units @ £24)						468,000
less Cost of sales:			Marginal			
	Units		cost			
Opening stock	3,000	@	£15	45,000		
add Production	21,000	@	£15	315,000		
	24,000	@	£15	360,000		
less Closing stock	4,500	@	£15	67,500		292,500*
Contribution**	19,500	@	£9			175,500
less Fixed costs					100,000	
Selling and distribution expenses					29,000	129,000
			Profit			£46,500

*The marginal cost of sales is 19,500 units @ £15 = £292,500
**The contribution per unit is selling price £24 less marginal cost £15 = £9

Figure A.3 Operating statement (marginal costing)

Table A.13 Absorption v. marginal: profit difference reconciliation

	Quarter to 31 March 19–4
Absorption costing profit	54,000
less Marginal costing profit	46,500
Difference	7,500
This is made up of the fixed overheads included in:	
	£
The closing stock of 4,500 units @ £5	22,500
less The opening stock of 3,000 units @ £5	15,000
Net stock increase 1,500 @ £5	7,500

Table A.14 Absorption v. marginal: alternative profit difference reconciliation

	Opening stock £	Closing stock £	Net stock Increase £
Absorption	60,000	90,000	30,000
Marginal	45,000	67,500	22,500
	15,000	22,500	7,500

Chapter 7: Pawilkes & Co. Ltd

Activity cost pools

Dept 1 (£000)	Dept 2 (£000)	Setting-up (£000)	Computing (£000)	Purchasing (£000)	Total (£000)
680	410	40	200	100	1430

Cost drivers (000)

340	410	10	40	50
Machine hrs	Direct lab. hrs	Set-ups	Computer hrs	Orders
£2 per machine hour	£1 per direct lab. hr	£4 per set-up	£5 per computer hour	£2 per order

Activity-based costing profit statement

	Product D		Product E	
Sales/production (units) (£000)	200,000		120,000	
	£	£	£	£
Sales		2,400		3,360
Less prime cost		1,600		2,160
		800		1,200
Cost pools:				
Dept. 1 @ £2 per machine hour	200		480	
Dept. 2 @ £1 per direct lab. hour	50		360	
Setting up @ £4 per set-up	24		16	
Computing @ £5 per computer hour	100		100	
Purchasing @ £2 per order	80	454	20	976
Profit		346		224

Total profit = £570,000

Chapter 8: Budgetary control self check

Budget

A budget has been defined by the CIMA (The Chartered Institute of Management Accountants) as:

> A plan expressed in money. It is prepared and approved prior to the budget period and may show income, expenditure, and the capital to be employed. May be drawn up showing incremental effects on former budgeted or actual figures, or be compiled by zero base budgeting.

Additional notes
You should note that a budget can be prepared in terms of quantity and/or value. For example, in practice, the production budget will first of all be drawn up in terms of quantity only. When it is clear that it coheres with the other budgets, e.g. sales, material requirements, labour requirements, etc., it will then be costed.

The keywords which you could have included in your own definition could include the following:

☐ It needs to be *predetermined/prepared in advance* of the period to which it relates.

☐ It aims at achieving specific *objectives*.

☐ It lays down the *policy* to be followed so that the objectives can be attained.

☐ In addition to budgeting income and expenditure it can also be used to budget the capital employed.

Budgetary control

Budgetary control has been defined by CIMA as:

> The establishment of budgets relating the responsibilities of executives to the requirements of a policy, and by continuous comparison of actual with budgeted results, either to secure by individual action the objectives of that policy or to provide a basis for its revision.

Additional notes

The keywords which you should have included in your definition are as follows:

☐ *Control by responsibility*.

☐ The *policy* to be followed.

☐ The *continuous comparison* of actual/budgeted figures, i.e. monitor at frequent intervals.

☐ *Management action* relating to the significant adverse variances, i.e. *management by exception*.

☐ The *attainment of the objectives*.

☐ The *revision* of the budget, if necessary, e.g. where basic assumptions change.

For both budgets and budgetary control I would also include:

☐ The involvement/participation of certain employees, e.g. supervisors.

☐ A common-sense approach, e.g. the setting of realistic and attainable targets.

☐ Consideration of the interrelationships between budgets.

☐ The importance of taking behavioural factors into account.

The principal budget factor

The principal budget factor (also known as the key factor or limiting factor) is the factor which must be taken into account first when budgeting, because it places a constraint upon the activities of a company/ organization. For example, if production capacity was limited in a certain period to 45,000 units it would be stupid to have a sales budget of 75,000 units. You cannot sell what you have not got! However, the principal budget factor (key factor/limiting factor) is not a fixed state of affairs and managers can by their actions eliminate it or reduce its effect. For example if production capacity was the limiting factor it could be increased by working shifts, buying more machines, using sub-contractors etc.

Control by responsibility

Control by responsibility in budgeting takes place when the responsibility for a budget/part of a budget is delegated to a particular person, who then becomes responsible for the achievement of the targets set. He or she has to explain to management the reasons why targets are not being achieved and the reasons for significant adverse variances. For example, a sales area manager will be responsible for the achievement of monthly sales targets in his/her area. In turn, each individual sales person would be responsible for their own monthly sales target.

Management by exception

This is a system which is designed to enable managers to use their time in a more productive/effective way. Reports and statements should highlight those items of significance which are *not* going according to plan. Managers will, therefore, devote a lot of time and effort into carefully reviewing such items and sorting out any necessary corrective action. They can devote their time and talents to those tasks which really need their undivided attention. It in effect directs, and in some ways forces managers to manage!

Chapter 8: The difference between profit and cash

The cash budget deals only with the actual cash which comes in or goes out during the period, i.e. the actual physical movement of cash. However, the trading and profit and loss account deals with items which are not included in the cash budget, which in the case of Brendug Co. Limited are as follows:

□ The sales figure of £88,000 represents the total sales made during the period irrespective of whether or not the cash has been received.

□ £66,000 is the total purchases figure for the period, i.e. it includes those which have been paid for in cash of £54,000 and those which have not yet been paid for of £12,000.

□ The closing stock of materials of £6,000. This is deducted in computing the cost of sales but does not affect the cash budget at all.

□ The charge for the use of plant and machinery, i.e. depreciation, charges a proportion of the cost in computing the loss.

Other comments

It must also be remembered that when profit is generated it is used to finance the purchase of fixed assets such as plant and machinery, fixtures and fittings, and to finance increases in the working capital, e.g. stocks and debtors. Thus, profit does not tend to stay cash for long, because the business spends it. Accrued and prepaid items will also be adjusted for in the profit and loss account but will not be adjusted for in the cash budget.

Chapter 8: Jeanles Ltd

See Tables A.15–A.17.

Comments (not part of the answer)

Note that during January and March the cash budget reveals an overdraft but this is covered by the current overdraft limit negotiated with the bank. Note also that the depreciation of £7,500 is for half a year. It was assumed that all the cash from the issue of the ordinary share capital would be received before January 19–4.

Chapter 9: Material variances

Material cost variance

This represents the difference between the actual cost of materials, £48,100, and the standard cost of the materials (for the actual level of activity, i.e. 8,000 units) of £48,000. Because the actual cost exceeded the standard cost by £100, this is an overspend, and classified as an adverse variance.

Material price variance

This is that part of the material cost variance which arises from paying an actual price for materials of £1.85 per kilo, which is different from the standard price of £2 per kilo which it was planned to pay. In the example used the difference of 15p per kilo less than standard represents a cost saving and is, therefore, classed as a favourable variance.

Table A.15 Jeanles Ltd: cash budget

| | Inflows | | | Outflows | | | | | |
	Opening balance £000	Share capital £000	Sales £000	Purchases £000	Rent £000	Wages & salaries £000	General expenses £000	Fixed assets £000	Closing balance £000
Jan		60	—	—	1.4	1	0.5	59	(1.9)
Feb	(1.9)		8	—		1	0.5		4.6
Mar	4.6		20	10		1	0.5	16	(2.9)
Apr	(2.9)		28	15	1.4	1	0.5		7.2
May	7.2		28	21		1	0.5		12.7
Jun	12.7		28	21		1	0.5		18.2
			112	67	2.8	6.0	3.0	75	
+ debtors (1 month)			28						
			140						
+ creditors (2 months)				42					
				109					

Table A.16   Jeanles Ltd: budgeted trading and profit and loss account

		£000	£000
	Sales		140
less	Cost of sales:		
	Opening stock	–	
add	Purchases	109	
		109	
less	Closing stock	4	105
	Gross profit (25% of sales)		35
less	Expenses:		
	Rent	2.8	
	Wages and salaries	6.0	
	General expenses	3.0	
	Depreciation (75 × 20%)		
	for half-year	7.5	19.3
	Net profit		15.7

Table A.17   Jeanles Ltd: budgeted balance sheet

		£000	£000
	Capital employed:		
	Issued ordinary share capital	60	
	Retained profit	15.7	75.7
	Employment of capital:		
	Fixed assets	75	
less	Depreciation	7.5	67.5
	Working capital:		
	Current assets		
	Stock	4	
	Debtors (one month)	28	
	Cash & bank (per cash		
	budget	18.2	
		50.2	
	Current liabilities:		
	Creditors (two months)	42	8.2
			75.7

The price variance can also be calculated as shown in Table A.18.

This is really saying that for every kilo of material used a price saving of 15p takes place.

Also note in the example that the figures used of £48,100 and £52,000 both use the same quantity, i.e. the actual quantity of 26,000 kilos. Only the prices are different, i.e. £1.85 per kilo and £2 per kilo.

Table A.18 The material price variance

	Standard price per kilo	£2.00
less	Actual price per kilo	£1.85
	Saving per kilo	£0.15

Actual materials used $\times$ price saving = £3,900 (favourable)
  (26,000 kilos   (15p)

Table A.19 The material usage variance

		kilos
	Standard quantity (for actual level of output) of materials	24,000
less	Actual quantity of materials used	26,000
	Excess usage	(2,000)

Excess usage $\times$ standard price = usage variance = £4,000
 (2,000 kilos)   (£2)   (adverse)

Material usage variance

That part of the material cost variance which results from using an actual quantity of materials which is different from the standard quantity of materials applicable to the actual level of activity/output. We can compute the usage variance as shown in Table A.19.

Thus, this variance has arisen because it takes more material than planned to produce the 8,000 units. Also note, in our example that both calculations use the same price figure, i.e. the standard price; only the quantities are different, i.e. 24,000 kilos standard and 26,000 kilos actual. The adverse usage variance could have been caused by buying a lower quality material at the lower price of £1.85 per kilo.

Chapter 9: Labour variances

Work sheet

See Table A.20.

Further proof of the two sub-variances are:

labour rate variance = (actual hours $\times$ rate increase)
                    (1950 $\times$ 50p) = £975 (adverse)

Table A.20   Standard costing: labour variance

	Labour cost variance £	Labour rate variance £	Labour efficiency variance £
Actual hours @ actual rate (1,950 @ £8.50)	16,575	16,575	–
Standard hours @ standard rate (2,000 @ £8)	16,000	–	16,000
Actual hours @ standard rate (1,950 @ £8)	–	15,600	15,600
	575	975	400
	(Adverse)	(Adverse)	(Favourable)

Summary (proof)		£
Labour rate variance	(Adverse)	(975)
Labour efficiency variance	Favourable	400
= Labour cost variance	(Adverse)	(575)

It is adverse, because the labour rate which was actually paid was 50p per hour more than the planned rate.

labour efficiency variance = actual hours less standard hours
$$(1,950) \qquad (2,000)$$
$$= 50 \text{ hours @ standard rate (£8)}$$
$$= £400 \text{ favourable}$$

This variance is favourable because the actual time taken to do the work was less than the standard time allowed. From a study of the answer, it can be observed that the labour cost variance (sometimes called the wages cost variance) is the difference between the actual hours spent producing the actual production of 1,000 units at the actual labour rate per hour, and the standard labour time allowed to produce (the actual production) 1,000 units at the standard labour rate per hour.

Chapter 10: The equivalent cash price

See Table A.21.

This represents the present value of the cash which will be paid out now and in the future. It also indicates the amount which would have to be invested now at 12% compound interest per annum to produce the instalments as and when they are needed, i.e. £14,803.5 less the delivery

Table A.21 The equivalent cash price via present value tables

	£
Payable on delivery (i.e. now)	3,000
The present value of an annuity of £3,000 for 3 years @ 12% (£3,000 × 2.402) (Table 10.8)	7,206
The present value of £5,000 in 4 years' time (£5,000 × 0.636) (Table 10.7)	3,180
The present value of £2,500 in 5 years' time (£2,500 × 0.567) (Table 10.7)	1,417.5
Equivalent cash price	14,803.5

payment of £3,000 will have to be invested at the outset. This would then produce £3,000 × 3 years = £9,000 plus £5,000 at the end of the fourth year and £2,500 at the end of the fifth year, a total of £16,500 (excluding the delivery payment).

Chapter 10: Identical cash flows/the treatment of depreciation

The NPV is negative, i.e. the discounted cash flows come to less than the initial investment; the project should not, therefore, go ahead (see Table A.22).

Note on depreciation

Depreciation is irrelevant: as it had not been deducted in computing the cash flows, no adjustment to the cash flows was necessary.

Table A.22 Identical cash flows/the treatment of depreciation

Annual cash flow £	Present value of an annuity of £1 for 6 years @ 16%*	Present value of cash flows £
12,000 ×	3.685	= 44,220
less Initial investment		60,000
Net present value		(15,780)

*As per Table 10.8.

Chapter 10: Becwik Ltd

See Table A.23.

The project has an NPV of £694,000 positive and is, therefore, worthy of consideration, i.e. it is acceptable according to the financial criteria. But non-financial considerations also need to be investigated. Note that the depreciation had not been deducted in computing the incremental cash flow and is therefore irrelevant.

Table A.23 Becwik Ltd: net present value

Year	Cash flow £000	Discount factor 14%	Present value £000
1	10	0.877	8.77
2	20	0.769	15.38
3	40	0.675	27.00
4	50	0.592	29.60
5	10	0.519	5.19
			85.94
		less Initial cost	79.00
		Net present value	**6.94**

Appendix 2

Present value tables and annuity tables

Appendix Table 1   Present value of £1 due at end of *n* years

n	1%	2%	3%	4%	5%	6%	7%	8%	9%	10%	n
1	0.99010	0.98039	0.97007	0.96154	0.95238	0.94340	0.93458	0.92593	0.91743	0.90909	1
2	0.98030	0.96117	0.94260	0.92456	0.90703	0.89000	0.87344	0.85734	0.84168	0.82645	2
3	0.97059	0.94232	0.91514	0.88900	0.86384	0.83962	0.81630	0.79383	0.77218	0.75131	3
4	0.96098	0.92385	0.88849	0.85480	0.82270	0.79209	0.76290	0.73503	0.70843	0.68301	4
5	0.95147	0.90573	0.86261	0.82193	0.78353	0.74726	0.71299	0.68058	0.64993	0.62092	5
6	0.94204	0.88797	0.83748	0.79031	0.74622	0.70496	0.66634	0.63017	0.59627	0.56447	6
7	0.93272	0.87056	0.81309	0.75992	0.71068	0.66506	0.62275	0.58349	0.54703	0.51316	7
8	0.92348	0.85349	0.78941	0.73069	0.67684	0.62741	0.58201	0.54027	0.50187	0.46651	8
9	0.91434	0.83675	0.76642	0.70259	0.64461	0.59190	0.54393	0.50025	0.46043	0.42410	9
10	0.90529	0.82035	0.74409	0.67556	0.61391	0.55839	0.50835	0.46319	0.42241	0.38554	10
11	0.89632	0.80426	0.72242	0.64958	0.58468	0.52679	0.47509	0.42888	0.38753	0.35049	11
12	0.88745	0.78849	0.70138	0.62460	0.55684	0.49697	0.44401	0.39711	0.35553	0.31863	12
13	0.87866	0.77303	0.68095	0.60057	0.53032	0.46884	0.41496	0.36770	0.32618	0.28966	13
14	0.86996	0.75787	0.66112	0.57747	0.50507	0.44230	0.38782	0.34046	0.29925	0.26333	14
15	0.86135	0.74301	0.64186	0.55526	0.48102	0.41726	0.36245	0.31524	0.27454	0.23939	15
16	0.85282	0.72845	0.62317	0.53391	0.45811	0.39365	0.33873	0.29189	0.25187	0.21763	16
17	0.84438	0.71416	0.60502	0.51337	0.43630	0.37136	0.31657	0.27027	0.23107	0.19784	17
18	0.83602	0.70016	0.58739	0.49363	0.41552	0.35034	0.29586	0.25025	0.21199	0.17986	18
19	0.82774	0.68643	0.57029	0.47464	0.39573	0.33051	0.27651	0.23171	0.19449	0.16351	19
20	0.81954	0.67297	0.55367	0.45639	0.37689	0.31180	0.25842	0.21455	0.17843	0.14864	20
21	0.81143	0.65978	0.53755	0.43883	0.35894	0.29415	0.24151	0.19866	0.16370	0.13513	21
22	0.80340	0.64684	0.52189	0.42195	0.34185	0.27750	0.22571	0.18394	0.15018	0.12285	22
23	0.79544	0.63414	0.50669	0.40573	0.32557	0.26180	0.21095	0.17031	0.13778	0.11168	23
24	0.78757	0.62172	0.49193	0.39012	0.31007	0.24698	0.19715	0.15770	0.12640	0.10153	24
25	0.77977	0.60953	0.47760	0.37512	0.29530	0.23300	0.18425	0.14602	0.11597	0.09230	25

Note: $PV = £1/(1 + r)^n$

Appendix Table 1 continued

n	11%	12%	13%	14%	15%	16%	17%	18%	19%	20%	n
1	0.90090	0.89286	0.88496	0.87719	0.86957	0.86207	0.85470	0.84746	0.84034	0.83333	1
2	0.81162	0.79719	0.78315	0.76947	0.75614	0.74316	0.73051	0.71818	0.70616	0.69444	2
3	0.73119	0.71178	0.69305	0.67497	0.65752	0.64066	0.62437	0.60863	0.59342	0.57870	3
4	0.65873	0.63552	0.61332	0.59208	0.57175	0.55229	0.53365	0.51579	0.49867	0.48225	4
5	0.59345	0.56743	0.54276	0.51937	0.49718	0.47611	0.45611	0.43711	0.41905	0.40188	5
6	0.53464	0.50663	0.48032	0.45559	0.43233	0.41044	0.38984	0.37043	0.35214	0.33490	6
7	0.48166	0.45235	0.42506	0.39964	0.37594	0.35383	0.33320	0.31392	0.29592	0.27908	7
8	0.43393	0.40388	0.37616	0.35056	0.32690	0.30503	0.28487	0.26604	0.24867	0.23257	8
9	0.39092	0.36061	0.33288	0.30751	0.28426	0.26295	0.24340	0.22546	0.20897	0.19381	9
10	0.35218	0.32197	0.29459	0.26974	0.24718	0.22668	0.20804	0.19106	0.17560	0.16151	10
11	0.31728	0.28748	0.26070	0.23662	0.21494	0.19542	0.17781	0.16192	0.14756	0.13459	11
12	0.28584	0.25667	0.23071	0.20756	0.18691	0.16846	0.15197	0.13722	0.12400	0.11216	12
13	0.25751	0.22917	0.20416	0.18207	0.16253	0.14523	0.12989	0.11629	0.10420	0.09346	13
14	0.23199	0.20462	0.18068	0.15971	0.14133	0.12520	0.11102	0.09855	0.08757	0.07789	14
15	0.20900	0.18270	0.15989	0.14010	0.12289	0.10793	0.09489	0.08352	0.07359	0.06491	15
16	0.18829	0.16312	0.14150	0.12289	0.10686	0.09304	0.08110	0.07078	0.06184	0.05409	16
17	0.16963	0.14564	0.12522	0.10780	0.09393	0.08021	0.06932	0.05998	0.05196	0.04507	17
18	0.15282	0.13004	0.11081	0.09456	0.08080	0.06914	0.05925	0.05083	0.04367	0.03756	18
19	0.13768	0.11611	0.09806	0.08295	0.07026	0.05961	0.05064	0.04308	0.03669	0.03130	19
20	0.12403	0.10367	0.08678	0.07276	0.06110	0.05139	0.04328	0.03651	0.03084	0.02608	20
21	0.11174	0.09256	0.07680	0.06383	0.05313	0.04430	0.03699	0.03094	0.02591	0.02174	21
22	0.10067	0.08264	0.06796	0.05599	0.04620	0.03819	0.03162	0.02622	0.02178	0.01811	22
23	0.09069	0.07379	0.06014	0.04911	0.04017	0.03292	0.02702	0.02222	0.01830	0.01509	23
24	0.08170	0.06588	0.05322	0.04308	0.03493	0.02838	0.02310	0.01883	0.01538	0.01258	24
25	0.07361	0.05882	0.04710	0.03779	0.03038	0.02447	0.01974	0.01596	0.01292	0.01048	25

Appendix Table 1 continued

n	21%	22%	23%	24%	25%	26%	27%	28%	29%	30%	n
1	0.82645	0.81967	0.81301	0.80645	0.80000	0.79365	0.78740	0.78125	0.77519	0.76923	1
2	0.68301	0.67186	0.66098	0.65036	0.64000	0.62988	0.62000	0.61035	0.60093	0.59172	2
3	0.56447	0.55071	0.53738	0.52449	0.51200	0.49991	0.48819	0.47684	0.46583	0.45517	3
4	0.46651	0.45140	0.43690	0.42297	0.40960	0.39675	0.38440	0.37253	0.36111	0.35013	4
5	0.38554	0.37000	0.35520	0.34111	0.32768	0.31488	0.30268	0.29104	0.27993	0.26933	5
6	0.31863	0.30328	0.28878	0.27509	0.26214	0.24991	0.23833	0.22737	0.21700	0.20718	6
7	0.26333	0.24859	0.23478	0.22184	0.20972	0.19834	0.18766	0.17764	0.16822	0.15937	7
8	0.21763	0.20376	0.19088	0.17891	0.16777	0.15741	0.14776	0.13878	0.13040	0.12259	8
9	0.17986	0.16702	0.15519	0.14428	0.13422	0.12493	0.11635	0.10842	0.10109	0.09430	9
10	0.14864	0.13690	0.12617	0.11635	0.10737	0.09915	0.09161	0.08470	0.07836	0.07254	10
11	0.12285	0.11221	0.10258	0.09383	0.08590	0.07869	0.07214	0.06617	0.06075	0.05580	11
12	0.10153	0.09198	0.08339	0.07567	0.06872	0.06245	0.05680	0.05170	0.04709	0.04292	12
13	0.08391	0.07539	0.06780	0.06103	0.05498	0.04957	0.04472	0.04039	0.03650	0.03302	13
14	0.06934	0.06180	0.05512	0.04921	0.04398	0.03934	0.03522	0.03155	0.02830	0.02540	14
15	0.05731	0.05065	0.04481	0.03969	0.03518	0.03122	0.02773	0.02465	0.02194	0.01954	15
16	0.04736	0.04152	0.03643	0.03201	0.02815	0.02478	0.02183	0.01926	0.01700	0.01503	16
17	0.03914	0.03403	0.02962	0.02581	0.02252	0.01967	0.01719	0.01505	0.01318	0.01156	17
18	0.03235	0.02789	0.02408	0.02082	0.01801	0.01561	0.01354	0.01175	0.01022	0.00889	18
19	0.02673	0.02286	0.01958	0.01679	0.01441	0.01239	0.01066	0.00918	0.00792	0.00684	19
20	0.02209	0.01874	0.01592	0.01354	0.01153	0.00983	0.00839	0.00717	0.00614	0.00526	20
21	0.01826	0.01536	0.01294	0.01092	0.00922	0.00780	0.00661	0.00561	0.00476	0.00405	21
22	0.01509	0.01259	0.01052	0.00880	0.00738	0.00619	0.00520	0.00438	0.00369	0.00311	22
23	0.01247	0.01032	0.00855	0.00710	0.00590	0.00491	0.00410	0.00342	0.00286	0.00239	23
24	0.01031	0.00846	0.00695	0.00573	0.00472	0.00390	0.00323	0.00267	0.00222	0.00184	24
25	0.00852	0.00693	0.00565	0.00462	0.00378	0.00310	0.00254	0.00209	0.00172	0.00152	25

Appendix Table 1 continued

n	31%	32%	33%	34%	35%	36%	37%	38%	39%	40%	n
1	0.76336	0.75758	0.75188	0.74627	0.74074	0.73529	0.72993	0.72464	0.71942	0.71429	1
2	0.58272	0.57392	0.56532	0.55692	0.54870	0.54066	0.53279	0.52510	0.51757	0.51020	2
3	0.44482	0.43479	0.42505	0.41561	0.40644	0.39754	0.38890	0.38051	0.37235	0.36443	3
4	0.33956	0.32939	0.31959	0.31016	0.30107	0.29231	0.28387	0.27573	0.26788	0.26031	4
5	0.25920	0.24953	0.24029	0.23146	0.22301	0.21493	0.20720	0.19980	0.19272	0.18593	5
6	0.19787	0.18904	0.18067	0.17273	0.16520	0.15804	0.15124	0.14479	0.13865	0.13281	6
7	0.15104	0.14321	0.13584	0.12890	0.12237	0.11621	0.11040	0.10492	0.09975	0.09486	7
8	0.11530	0.10849	0.10214	0.09620	0.09064	0.08545	0.08058	0.07603	0.07176	0.06776	8
9	0.08802	0.08219	0.07680	0.07179	0.06714	0.06283	0.05882	0.05509	0.05163	0.04840	9
10	0.06719	0.06227	0.05774	0.05357	0.04973	0.04620	0.04293	0.03992	0.03714	0.03457	10
11	0.05129	0.04717	0.04341	0.03998	0.03684	0.03397	0.03134	0.02893	0.02672	0.02469	11
12	0.03915	0.03574	0.03264	0.02984	0.02729	0.02498	0.02287	0.02096	0.01922	0.01764	12
13	0.02989	0.02707	0.02454	0.02227	0.02021	0.01837	0.01670	0.01519	0.01383	0.01260	13
14	0.02281	0.02051	0.01845	0.01662	0.01497	0.01350	0.01219	0.01101	0.00995	0.00900	14
15	0.01742	0.01554	0.01387	0.01240	0.01109	0.00993	0.00890	0.00798	0.00716	0.00643	15
16	0.01329	0.01177	0.01043	0.00925	0.00822	0.00730	0.00649	0.00578	0.00515	0.00459	16
17	0.01015	0.00892	0.00784	0.00691	0.00609	0.00537	0.00474	0.00419	0.00370	0.00328	17
18	0.00775	0.00676	0.00590	0.00515	0.00451	0.00395	0.00346	0.00304	0.00267	0.00234	18
19	0.00591	0.00512	0.00443	0.00385	0.00334	0.00290	0.00253	0.00220	0.00192	0.00167	19
20	0.00451	0.00388	0.00333	0.00287	0.00247	0.00213	0.00184	0.00159	0.00138	0.00120	20
21	0.00345	0.00294	0.00251	0.00214	0.00183	0.00157	0.00135	0.00115	0.00099	0.00085	21
22	0.00263	0.00223	0.00188	0.00160	0.00136	0.00115	0.00098	0.00084	0.00071	0.00061	22
23	0.00201	0.00169	0.00142	0.00119	0.00101	0.00085	0.00072	0.00061	0.00051	0.00044	23
24	0.00153	0.00128	0.00107	0.00089	0.00074	0.00062	0.00052	0.00044	0.00037	0.00031	24
25	0.00117	0.00097	0.00080	0.00066	0.00055	0.00046	0.00038	0.00032	0.00027	0.00022	25

Appendix Table 2 Present value of an annuity of £1 for n years

n	1%	2%	3%	4%	5%	6%	7%	8%	9%	10%	n
1	0.9901	0.9804	0.9709	0.9615	0.9524	0.9434	0.9346	0.9259	0.9174	0.9091	1
2	1.9704	1.9416	1.9135	1.8861	1.8594	1.8334	1.8080	1.7833	1.7591	1.7355	2
3	2.9410	2.8839	2.8286	2.7751	2.7232	2.6730	2.6243	2.5771	2.5313	2.4868	3
4	3.9020	3.8077	3.7171	3.6299	3.5459	3.4651	3.3872	3.3121	3.2397	3.1699	4
5	4.8535	4.7134	4.5797	4.4518	4.3295	4.2124	4.1002	3.9927	3.8896	3.7908	5
6	5.7955	5.6014	5.4172	5.2421	5.0757	4.9173	4.7665	4.6229	4.4859	4.3553	6
7	6.7282	6.4720	6.2302	6.0020	5.7863	5.5824	5.3893	5.2064	5.0329	4.8684	7
8	7.6517	7.3254	7.0196	6.7327	6.4632	6.2098	5.9713	5.7466	5.5348	5.3349	8
9	8.5661	8.1622	7.7861	7.4353	7.1078	6.8017	6.5152	6.2469	5.9852	5.7590	9
10	9.4714	8.9825	8.5302	8.1109	7.7217	7.3601	7.0236	6.7101	6.4176	6.1446	10
11	10.3677	9.7868	9.2526	8.7604	8.3064	7.8868	7.4987	7.1389	6.8052	6.4951	11
12	11.2552	10.5753	9.9539	9.3850	8.8632	8.3838	7.9427	7.5361	7.1607	6.8137	12
13	12.1338	11.3483	10.6349	9.9856	9.3935	8.8527	8.3576	7.9038	7.4869	7.1034	13
14	13.0038	12.1062	11.2960	10.5631	9.8986	9.2950	8.7454	8.2442	7.7861	7.3667	14
15	13.8651	12.8492	11.9379	11.1183	10.3796	9.7122	9.1079	8.5595	8.0607	7.6061	15
16	14.7180	13.5777	12.5610	11.6522	10.8377	10.1059	9.4466	8.8514	8.3125	7.8237	16
17	15.5624	14.2918	13.1660	12.1656	11.2740	10.4772	9.7632	9.1216	8.5436	8.0215	17
18	16.3984	14.9920	13.7534	12.6592	11.6895	10.8276	10.0591	9.3719	8.7556	8.2014	18
19	17.2261	15.6784	14.3237	13.1339	12.0853	11.1581	10.3356	9.6036	8.9501	8.3649	19
20	18.0457	16.3514	14.8774	13.5903	12.4622	11.4699	10.5940	9.8181	9.1285	8.5136	20
21	18.8571	17.0111	15.4149	14.0291	12.8211	11.7640	10.8355	10.0168	9.2922	8.6487	21
22	19.6605	17.6580	15.9368	14.4511	13.1630	12.0416	11.0612	10.2007	9.4424	8.7715	22
23	20.4559	18.2921	16.4435	14.8568	13.4885	12.3033	11.2722	10.3710	9.5802	8.8832	23
24	21.2435	18.9139	16.9355	15.2469	13.7986	12.5503	11.4693	10.5287	9.7066	8.9847	24
25	22.0233	19.5234	17.4131	15.6220	14.0939	12.7833	11.6536	10.6748	9.8226	9.0770	25

Appendix Table 2 continued

n	11%	12%	13%	14%	15%	16%	17%	18%	19%	20%	n
1	0.0009	0.8929	0.8850	0.3772	0.8696	0.8621	0.8547	0.8475	0.8403	0.8333	1
2	1.7125	1.6901	1.6681	1.6467	1.6257	1.6052	1.5852	1.5656	1.5465	1.5278	2
3	2.4437	2.4018	2.3612	2.3216	2.2832	2.2459	2.2096	2.1743	2.1399	2.1065	3
4	3.1024	3.0373	2.9745	2.9137	2.8550	2.7982	2.7432	2.6901	2.6386	2.5887	4
5	3.6959	3.6048	3.5172	3.4331	3.3522	3.2743	3.1993	3.1272	3.0576	2.9906	5
6	4.2305	4.1114	3.9976	3.8887	3.7845	3.6847	3.5892	3.4976	3.4098	3.3255	6
7	4.7122	4.5638	4.4226	4.2883	4.1604	4.0386	3.9224	3.8115	3.7057	3.6046	7
8	5.1461	4.9676	4.7988	4.6389	4.4873	4.3436	4.2072	4.0776	3.9544	3.8372	8
9	5.5370	5.3282	5.1317	4.9464	4.7716	4.6065	4.4506	4.3030	4.1633	4.0310	9
10	5.8892	5.6502	5.4262	5.2161	5.0188	4.8332	4.6586	4.4941	4.3389	4.1925	10
11	6.2065	5.9377	5.6869	5.4527	5.2337	5.0286	4.8364	4.6560	4.4865	4.3271	11
12	6.4924	6.1944	5.9176	5.6603	5.4206	5.1971	4.9884	4.7932	4.6105	4.4392	12
13	6.7499	6.4235	6.1218	5.8424	5.5931	5.3423	5.1183	4.9095	4.7147	4.5327	13
14	6.9819	6.6282	6.3025	6.0021	5.7245	5.4675	5.2293	5.0081	4.8023	4.6106	14
15	7.1909	6.8109	6.4624	6.1422	5.8474	5.5755	5.3242	5.0916	4.8759	4.6755	15
16	7.3792	6.9740	6.6039	6.2651	5.9542	5.6685	5.4053	5.1624	4.9377	4.7296	16
17	7.5488	7.1196	6.7291	6.3729	6.0472	5.7487	5.4746	5.2223	4.9897	4.7746	17
18	7.7016	7.2497	6.8399	6.4674	6.1280	5.8178	5.5339	5.2732	5.0333	4.8122	18
19	7.8393	7.3658	6.9380	6.5504	6.1982	5.8775	5.5845	5.3162	5.0700	4.8435	19
20	7.9633	7.4694	7.0248	6.6231	6.2593	5.9288	5.6278	5.3527	5.1009	4.8696	20
21	8.0751	7.5620	7.1016	6.6870	6.3125	5.9731	5.6648	5.3837	5.1268	4.8913	21
22	8.1757	7.6446	7.1695	6.7429	6.3587	6.0113	5.6964	5.4099	5.1486	4.9094	22
23	8.2664	7.7184	7.2297	6.7921	6.3988	6.0442	5.7234	5.4321	5.1668	4.9245	23
24	8.3481	7.7843	7.2829	6.8351	6.4338	6.0726	5.7465	5.4509	5.1822	4.9371	24
25	8.4217	7.8431	7.3300	6.8729	6.4641	6.0971	5.7662	5.4669	5.1951	4.9476	25

Appendix Table 2 continued

n	21%	22%	23%	24%	25%	26%	27%	28%	29%	30%	n
1	0.8264	0.8197	0.8130	0.8065	0.8000	0.7937	0.7874	0.7813	0.7752	0.7592	1
2	1.5095	1.4915	1.4740	1.4568	1.4400	1.4235	1.4074	1.3916	1.3761	1.3609	2
3	2.0738	2.0422	2.0114	1.9813	1.9520	1.9234	1.8956	1.8684	1.8420	1.8161	3
4	2.5404	2.4936	2.4483	2.4043	2.3616	2.3202	2.2800	2.2410	2.2031	2.1662	4
5	2.9260	2.8636	2.8035	2.7454	2.6893	2.6351	2.5827	2.5320	2.4830	2.4356	5
6	3.2446	3.1669	3.0923	3.0205	2.9514	2.8850	2.8210	2.7594	2.7000	2.6427	6
7	3.5079	3.4155	3.3270	3.2423	3.1611	3.0833	3.0087	2.9370	2.8682	2.8021	7
8	3.7256	3.6193	3.5179	3.4212	3.3289	3.2407	3.1564	3.0758	2.9986	2.9247	8
9	3.9054	3.7863	3.6731	3.5655	3.4631	3.3657	3.2728	3.1842	3.0997	3.0190	9
10	4.0541	3.9232	3.7993	3.6819	3.5705	3.4648	3.3644	3.2689	3.1781	3.0915	10
11	4.1769	4.0354	3.9018	3.7757	3.6564	3.5435	3.4365	3.3351	3.2388	3.1473	11
12	4.2785	4.1274	3.9852	3.8514	3.7251	3.6060	3.4933	3.3868	3.2859	3.1903	12
13	4.3624	4.2028	4.0530	3.9124	3.7801	3.6555	3.5381	3.4272	3.3224	3.2233	13
14	4.4317	4.2646	4.1082	3.9616	3.8241	3.6949	3.5733	3.4587	3.3507	3.2487	14
15	4.4890	4.3152	4.1530	4.0013	3.8593	3.7261	3.6010	3.4834	3.3726	3.2682	15
16	4.5364	4.3567	4.1894	4.0333	3.8874	3.7509	3.6228	3.5026	3.3896	3.2832	16
17	4.5755	4.3908	4.2190	4.0591	3.9099	3.7705	3.6400	3.5177	3.4028	3.2948	17
18	4.6079	4.4187	4.2431	4.0799	3.9279	3.7861	3.6536	3.5294	3.4130	3.3037	18
19	4.6346	4.4415	4.2627	4.0967	3.9424	3.7985	3.6642	3.5386	3.4210	3.3105	19
20	4.6567	4.4603	4.2786	4.1103	3.9539	3.8083	3.6726	3.5458	3.4271	3.3158	20
21	4.6750	4.4756	4.2916	4.1212	3.9631	3.8161	3.6792	3.5514	3.4319	3.3198	21
22	4.6900	4.4882	4.3021	4.1300	3.9705	3.8223	3.6844	3.5558	3.4356	3.3230	22
23	4.7025	4.4985	4.3106	4.1371	3.9764	3.8273	3.6885	3.5592	3.4384	3.3254	23
24	4.7128	4.5070	4.3176	4.1428	3.9811	3.8312	3.6918	3.5619	3.4406	3.3272	24
25	4.7213	4.5139	4.3232	4.1474	3.9849	3.8342	3.6943	3.5640	3.4423	3.3286	25

Appendix Table 2 continued

n	31%	32%	33%	34%	35%	36%	37%	38%	39%	40%	n
1	0.7634	0.7576	0.7519	0.7463	0.7407	0.7353	0.7299	0.7246	0.7194	0.7143	1
2	1.3461	1.3315	1.3172	1.3032	1.2894	1.2760	1.2627	1.2497	1.2370	1.2245	2
3	1.7909	1.7663	1.7423	1.7188	1.6959	1.6735	1.6516	1.6302	1.6093	1.5889	3
4	2.1305	2.0957	2.0618	2.0290	1.9969	1.9658	1.9355	1.9060	1.8772	1.8492	4
5	2.3897	2.3452	2.3021	2.2604	2.2200	2.1807	2.1427	2.1058	2.0699	1.9352	5
6	2.5875	2.5342	2.4828	2.4331	2.3852	2.3388	2.2936	2.2506	2.2086	2.1680	6
7	2.7386	2.6775	2.6187	2.5620	2.5075	2.4550	2.4043	2.3555	2.3083	2.2628	7
8	2.8539	2.7860	2.7208	2.6582	2.5982	2.5404	2.4849	2.4315	2.3801	2.3306	8
9	2.9419	2.8681	2.7976	2.7300	2.6653	2.6033	2.5437	2.4866	2.4317	2.3790	9
10	3.0091	2.9304	2.8553	2.7836	2.7150	2.6495	2.5867	2.5265	2.4689	2.4136	10
11	3.0604	2.9776	2.8987	2.8236	2.7519	2.6834	2.6180	2.5555	2.4956	2.4383	11
12	3.0995	3.0133	2.9314	2.8534	2.7792	2.7084	2.6409	2.5764	2.5148	2.4559	12
13	3.1294	3.0404	2.9559	2.8757	2.7994	2.7268	2.6576	2.5916	2.5286	2.4685	13
14	3.1522	3.0609	2.9744	2.8923	2.8144	2.7403	2.6698	2.6026	2.5386	2.4775	14
15	3.1696	3.0764	2.9883	2.9047	2.8255	2.7502	2.6787	2.6106	2.5457	2.4839	15
16	3.1829	3.0882	2.9987	2.9140	2.8337	2.7575	2.6852	2.6164	2.5509	2.4885	16
17	3.1931	3.0971	3.0065	2.9209	2.8398	2.7629	2.6899	2.6202	2.5546	2.4918	17
18	3.2008	3.1039	3.0124	2.9260	2.8443	2.7668	2.6934	2.6236	2.5573	2.4941	18
19	3.2067	3.1090	3.0169	2.9299	2.8476	2.7697	2.6959	2.6258	2.5592	2.4958	19
20	3.2112	3.1129	3.0202	2.9327	2.8501	2.7718	2.6977	2.6274	2.5606	2.4970	20
21	3.2174	3.1158	3.0227	2.9349	2.8519	2.7734	2.6991	2.6285	2.5616	2.4979	21
22	3.2173	3.1180	3.0246	2.9365	2.8533	2.7746	2.7000	2.6294	2.5623	2.4985	22
23	3.2193	3.1197	3.0260	2.9377	2.8543	2.7754	2.7008	2.6300	2.5628	2.4989	23
24	3.2209	3.1210	3.0271	2.9386	2.8550	2.7760	2.7013	2.6304	2.5632	2.4992	24
25	3.2220	3.1220	3.0279	2.9392	2.8556	2.7765	2.7017	2.6307	2.5634	2.4994	25

Index